CONTENTS

ACKNOWLEDGMENTS

There are many friends and loved ones to thank for their support of this humble project: my wife Laura and our children, Jean-Paul, Caroline, and Kimberley, for their constant love and support, *sine quā nōn* . . . ; Mary Wells Ricks, for her careful work on the manuscript itself, her judicious editorial advice, her friendship, and her unequaled good cheer; former graduate student Catherine Anne Bilow, dear friend as well, for her ever meticulous and enthusiastic research assistance; the many Latin teachers and professors who have field-tested portions of the book in their classes (Edith Black, Bob Burgess, Tom Curtis, Sally Davis, Tim Gantz, Muriel Garcia, Ellen Harris, Gail Polk, and Alysa Ward); Gil Lawall, for his masterful supervision of the Longman Latin Readers series; the outside readers, Margaret Brucia and Peter Howard, for saving me from many errors (those that remain, as they say, *omnēs meī sunt*) and for making this a better book in countless respects; the good folks at Longman, especially Lyn McLean, Aerin Csigay, Janice Baillie, and Winnie Jamison, for their steadfast encouragement and professionalism; the students in my spring, 1994, Ovid class (Amy Arthur, Angela Culpepper, David Hill, Charles McKinley, and Natalie Wilson), for their very helpful suggestions; and others at the University of Georgia who have assisted in important ways, among them Frances Van Keuren, Marshall Lloyd, Connie Russell, Dean Wyatt W. Anderson, and Vice President for Research Joe L. Key.

My most obvious debt, of course, is to Naso himself for what Sir Samuel Garth so elegantly termed (in the preface to his 1711 translation of the *Metamorphoses*) the poet's "infinite variety of inimitable excellencies," an artistry and a passion that have provided me such pleasure these many months. And lastly, with Ovid himself, may I say

IVRE TIBI GRATES, CANDIDE LECTOR, AGO

Tristia, IV.10.132

* * *

Photo Credits: Cover and pages 1, 30, 75, 108, 119, 127, 134, Alinari/Art Resource, NY; page 35, Bridgeman/Art Resource, NY; page 118, Cameraphoto/Art Resource, NY; pages 4, 55, 89, Giraudon/Art Resource, NY; page 57, Foto Marburg/Art Resource, NY; pages 77 (gift of Thomas F. Ryan, 1910), 88 (gift of Louis C. Raegner, 1927), Metropolitan Museum of Art; page 31, Abby Aldrich Rockefeller Fund, Museum of Modern Art, New York; page 99, Walters Art Gallery, Baltimore; page 126, from A. Baumeister, *Denkmäler des klassischen Altertums* (Munich GER: Oldenbourg, 1885), page 316.

Text Credits: The Latin text has been newly edited, with attention to punctuation, capitalization, and paragraphing, as well as to manuscript variants listed in the principal editions; most frequently consulted were William S. Anderson, ed., *Ovidius: Metamorphoses* (Leipzig GER: Teubner, 1985) and E.J. Kenney, ed., *P. Ovidi Nasonis: Amores, Medicamina Faciei Femineae, Ars Amatoria, Remedia Amoris* (Oxford ENG: Oxford University Press, 1968). Poems by A. E. Stallings, pages 5 and 31, were previously published in, respectively, *Classical Association News* and *The Beloit Poetry Journal*.

LOVE AND TRANSFORMATION

An Ovid Reader

RICHARD A. LaFLEUR
The University of Georgia

Addison-Wesley Publishing Company
Reading, Massachusetts • Menlo Park, California
New York • Don Mills, Ontario • Wokingham, England
Amsterdam • Bonn • Sydney • Singapore • Tokyo
Madrid • San Juan • Paris • Seoul, Korea • Milan
Mexico City • Taipei, Taiwan

Love and Transformation: An Ovid Reader

Series Editor: Professor Gilbert Lawall, University of Massachusetts, Amherst, MA
Consultants: Dr. Margaret A. Brucia, Earl Vandermeulen High School, Port Jefferson, NY
               Professor Peter Howard, Troy State University, Troy, AL

Executive editor: Lyn McLean
Production editor: Janice L. Baillie
Cover design: Curt Belshe
Photo cover and page 1: "Apollo and Daphne,"
  Gian Lorenzo Bernini, 1624, Villa Borghese,
  Rome; Alinari/Art Resource, NY
Photo research: Aerin Csigay

Photo/text credits appear on page iv

ISBN: 0-8013-1299-X

6 7 8 9 10-VG-00999897

quī dare certa ferae, dare vulnera possumus hostī,
quī modo, pestiferō tot iūgera ventre prementem,
460 strāvimus innumerīs tumidum Pȳthōna sagittīs.
Tū face nescio quōs estō contentus amōrēs
irrītāre tuā nec laudēs assere nostrās."
Fīlius huic Veneris "Fīgat tuus omnia, Phoebe,
tē meus arcus" ait, "quantōque animālia cēdunt
465 cūncta deō, tantō minor est tua glōria nostra."

Discussion Questions

1. How do the tale's opening lines (452–62) employ military imagery to anticipate the conflict between Cupid and Apollo?

2. What is the tone of Apollo's speech to Cupid (454–62) and what initial impression does it give you of the god's character?

3. What is the effect of the chiasmus in 463–64?

---

asserō, asserere, asseruī, assertus, *to lay claim to, claim as one's own* (like **estō**, the verb has a legalistic sense—Apollo is "laying down the law").
nostrās: i.e., *that are owed to us (me)*.
463 *Venus, Veneris, f., *Venus* (goddess of love and Cupid's mother).
*fīgō, fīgere, fīxī, fīxus, *to drive in, insert; to transfix, pierce; to fix, press*.
Fīgat . . . arcus (464): verb and subject neatly frame the purposely elliptical clause; the full expression would be **Tuus arcus omnia fīgat et meus arcus tē fīgat**.
tuus omnia . . . / tē meus (464): chiasmus.
464 *arcus, -ūs, m., *a bow*.
ait: with direct quotes the speech verb is often delayed (cf. **dīxerat** 457), but it should usually be translated with the subject and before the quotation (**Fīlius . . . Veneris . . . ait**, *the son of Venus says*).
quantō . . . tantō (465): *by as much as . . . by that much* (abl. of degree of difference).
animal, animālis, n., *an animal, any living thing* (including men as well as beasts, and even plants).
*cēdō, cēdere, cessī, cessūrus, *to go, proceed*; + dat., *to yield to, be inferior to*.
465 nostrā: sc. **glōriā**; abl. of comparison. The word deliberately, and contemptuously, echoes the identically positioned **nostrās** (462).

466   **Dīxit**: often used to mark the end of a direct quotation.
  ēlīdō, ēlīdere, ēlīsī, ēlīsus, *to break, shatter, crash through*.
  ***percutiō, percutere, percussī, percussus**, *to strike; to beat, shake violently*.
  ***āēr, āeris**, m., *air*.
  ***penna, -ae**, f., *a wing; a feather*.
    ēlīsō percussīs āere pennīs: an elaborate abl. absolute; freely, *crashing
    through the air with his beating wings*. The interlocked word order,
    with the violent participles first, then the nouns, suits the image of
    wings beating wildly through the air, and the s/-īs soundplay adds an
    onomatopoetic effect.

467   **impiger, impigra, impigrum**, *quick, swift* (here, with adverbial force,
  swiftly).
  umbrōsus, -a, -um, *shady*.
  Parnāsus, -ī, m., *Parnassus* (a mountain in Phocis, site of the holy city of
  Phocis and sacred to the Muses and Apollo).
  ***cōnstō, cōnstāre, cōnstitī, cōnstātūrus**, *to take up a position, stand upon,
  stand firmly*.
  arx, arcis, f., *citadel; hilltop, summit*.
    arce: sc. **in**, and note that prepositions common in prose are frequently
    omitted in verse.

468   **ēque**: **ē + que**.
  sagittiferus, -a, -um, *arrow-bearing* (cf. **sagittīs** 460).
  prōmō, prōmere, prōmpsī, prōmptus, *to bring forth, pull out*.
  tēlum, -ī, n., *weapon*.
  ***pharetra, -ae**, f., *quiver*.
    sagittiferā . . . duo tēla pharetrā: through a sort of chiastic word-
    picture, the arrows—or rather the words representing them, **duo
    tēla**—are actually "contained" within the quiver (and see on **innumerīs
    . . . sagittīs** 460).

469   ***dīversus, -a, -um**, *opposite; different; separate*.
  ***opus, operis**, n., *work, task; function, purpose*; **opus est** + abl., idiom,
  there is need of (something).
  ***fugō, -āre, -āvī, -ātus**, *to drive away, dispel, banish*.
  amōrem: object of both the preceding parallel phrases (which are in turn
  echoed in the opening phrases of 470 and 471).

470   **Quod facit . . . / quod fugat** (471): understand **tēlum** as antecedent and
  amōrem as object of both clauses, each of which is followed by a strong
  diaeresis setting up the contrasting images. The contrast is further
  underscored through the anaphora and soundplay in **quod facit/quod fugat**
  (the verbs sound alike but have opposite meanings) and the chiasmus in
  aurātum . . . acūtā / . . . obtūsum . . . plumbum (471).
  ***aurātus, -a, -um**, *golden*.
  ***cuspis, cuspidis**, f., *sharp point, tip*.
  fulgeō, fulgēre, fulsī, fulsūrus, *to shine brightly, gleam*.
  ***acūtus, -a, -um**, *sharp, pointed* (cf. *Am.* I.1.11).

471   **obtūsus, -a, -um**, *blunt, dull*.

Dīxit et, ēlīsō percussīs āere pennīs,
impiger umbrōsā Parnāsī cōnstitit arce,
ēque sagittiferā prōmpsit duo tēla pharetrā
dīversōrum operum. Fugat hoc, facit illud amōrem;
470   quod facit, aurātum est et cuspide fulget acūtā,
quod fugat, obtūsum est et habet sub harundine plumbum.
Hoc deus in nymphā Pēnēide fīxit, at illō
laesit Apollineās trāiecta per ossa medullās.

Discussion Questions

1.   In what ways may the interaction of Cupid and Apollo in the opening scene (through verse 473) be regarded as allegorical? I.e., what broader, symbolic point is conveyed to the reader in Cupid's victory over Apollo?

2.   Comment on the word order in 473 and its appropriateness to the sense of the verse.

---

    sub: here, perhaps because arrows were generally stored tip downward in the quiver and then held with the tip downward until shot, *(down) at the tip of.*
    harundō, harundinis, f., *a reed; the shaft of an arrow.*
    *****plumbum, -ī**, n., *lead.*
        The sound effects, especially alliteration of **b** and the **-um/-un/-um-/-um** assonance, are aptly dull and leaden, in contrast to the harsher **c/g** alliteration used in describing the sharp arrow in the preceding verse.
472   **Hoc . . . illō**: the words (*the latter . . . the former*) are placed at the ends of the line to further emphasize the contrast between the two arrows.
    illō / . . . Apollineās . . . medullās (473): a neat, lilting alliteration, underscored through the placement of **illō** and **medullās** at lines' end.
    *****Pēnēis, Pēnēidos**, abl. sing. **Pēnēide**, voc. sing. **Pēnēi**, acc. pl. **Pēnēidas**, *of the river Peneus, descended from the river-god Peneus;* here, *daughter of Peneus* (see on 452). For the patronymic form and Greek case-endings, see on **Bēlis** (X.44 below).
473   *****laedō, laedere, laesī, laesus**, *to harm, hurt, wound.*
    Apollineus, -a, -um, *of Apollo.*
    trāiciō, trāicere, trāiēcī, trāiectus, *to throw across; to transfix, pierce.*
    medulla, -ae, f., usually pl., *the marrow of the bones* (often used, as in English, of one's innermost soul and emotions).

474 ***prōtinus**, adv., *immediately*.
    alter amat, fugit altera: chiasmus again underscores the opposing actions.
    nōmen amantis: *the very word "lover"* (lit., *the name of a lover*).

475 **latebra, -ae**, f., often pl., *hiding place; refuge*.
    latebrīs . . . / exuviīs (476): sc. **in**, with **gaudēns**.
    *captīvus, -a, -um, *captured, captive*.

476 **exuviae, -ārum**, f. pl., *armor, spoils; the hide stripped from a beast*.
    innūptus, -a, -um, *unwed, maiden*.
    aemula, -ae, f., *a (female) rival*.
    *Phoebē, Phoebēs, f., *Diana* (sister of Phoebus Apollo and virgin goddess of the moon, wild animals, and woodlands).
        For the root meaning of the name, see on **Phoebus** 452; and for the word's Greek case endings (here gen.), cf. **Daphnē** 452.

477 **coerceō, -ēre, -uī, -itus**, *to restrain, confine; to hold back*.
    positōs: i.e., **dispositōs** (in poetry the simple form of a verb was often used in place of a compound), *arranged*.
    *lēx, lēgis, f., *law; rule, regulation, order*.
    sine lēge: i.e., *carelessly*; cf. the description of Daphne's hair at 497.

478 **illam petiēre; illa . . . petentēs**: anaphora; this and the three quick elisions suggest how abruptly Daphne rejected all suitors.
    petiēre: for **petīvērunt**; the alternative 3rd pers. pl. perf. ending **-ēre** is common in Latin verse, as are perf. system forms with the intervocalic **-v-** omitted (cf. **fīnierat** 566 for **fīnīverat**, and **agitāsse** 567 for **agitāvisse**).
    āversor, -ārī, -ātus sum, *to turn away from; to reject*.

479 **impatiēns, impatientis** + gen., *impatient or intolerant (of)*.
    expers, expertis + gen., *inexperienced (with), without knowledge (of)*.
    virī: construe with both preceding adjectives.
    nemus, nemoris, n., *woodland, forest; (sacred) grove*.
    āvius, -a, -um, *pathless, unfrequented; remote*.
    lūstrō, -āre, -āvī, -ātus, *to move around; to wander through, roam*.

480 **quid . . . quid . . . quid**: anaphora and asyndeton accentuate the series; the indirect questions, with **sint**, depend upon **cūrat**.
    Hymēn, Hymēnis, m., *a refrain shouted at weddings; marriage;* often, and probably here (with **Amor**), *Hymen* (the god of marriage—cf. X.2 below).
    Amor: Ovid refers not just to love, but to Cupid himself, who as god of love was often called Amor (cf. 532).
    *cōnūbium, -ī, n., often pl. for sing., *marriage, wedding rites*.

481 **gener, generī**, m., *son-in-law*.

482 **saepe pater dīxit**: the anaphora suits the point explicit in **saepe**; likewise the repetitions and chiastic arrangement of **"Generum mihi, fīlia, dēbēs";** / **. . . "Dēbēs mihi, nāta, nepōtēs"** suggest Peneus' insistent tone.
    nāta, -ae, f., *daughter*.
    nepōs, nepōtis, m./f., *a grandchild; descendant*.

483 **velut**, adv., often introducing similes, *just as, just like; as if, as though (it were)*.

Prōtinus alter amat, fugit altera nōmen amantis,
475 silvārum latebrīs captīvārumque ferārum
exuviīs gaudēns, innūptaeque aemula Phoebēs;
vitta coercēbat positōs sine lēge capillōs.
Multī illam petiēre; illa, āversāta petentēs
impatiēns expersque virī, nemora āvia lustrat,
480 nec, quid Hymēn, quid Amor, quid sint cōnūbia, cūrat.
Saepe pater dīxit, "Generum mihi, fīlia, dēbēs";
saepe pater dīxit, "Dēbēs mihi, nāta, nepōtēs."
Illa, velut crīmen taedās exōsa iugālēs,
pulchra verēcundō suffunditur ōra rubōre,

Discussion Question

What is the significance of Daphne's emulation of Diana (474–80) and how, in the context of this story, is it ironic?

---

*crīmen, crīminis, n., *charge, accusation; misdeed, crime.*
exōsus, -a, -um + acc., *hating, detesting.*
iugālis, -is, -e, *of marriage, matrimonial, nuptial.*
 taedās . . . iugālēs: by metonymy, *marriage*; torches were carried by the celebrants in Roman weddings.
484 **pulchra . . . rubōre**: note the line's interlocked word order and axial symmetry, with the adjectives preceding, the verb at center, and the nouns following (A¹ A² V N¹ N²)—sometimes called a "golden line," the arrangement was a favorite of Ovid's (cf. 528–29 and X.22 below).
verēcundus, -a, -um, *modest, chaste.*
suffundō, suffundere, suffūdī, suffūsus, *to pour on; to cover, fill.*
ōra: acc. of respect or specification, a Greek construction commonly used in Latin verse, especially of parts of the body; *her face is covered* (lit., *she is covered with respect to her face*). The pl. of ōs was often used for the sing. in verse.
rubor, rubōris, f., *blush.*

485   **inque . . . lacertīs**: interlocked order again—take **in** and **patris** with **cervīce**, and **blandīs** with **lacertīs**.

    *__blandus, -a, -um__, *coaxing, flattering; persuasive, enticing.*

        blandīs . . . lacertīs: a transferred epithet, as it is not, strictly speaking, her arms, but Daphne herself who coaxes her father into a change of heart.

    *__cervīx, cervīcis__, f., often pl. for sing., *the neck.*

    *__lacertus, -ī__, m., *the arm,* especially *the upper arm* (as in an embrace—cf. 501).

486   **perpetuā**: with **virginitāte** (487).

    *__genitor, genitōris__, m., *father, creator.*

    cārissime: Daphne's words as well as her embraces are designed to persuade.

487   **virginitās, virginitātis**, f., virginity, maidenhood.

        virginitāte fruī: Daphne's entreaty is given special point through enjambement and the heavy pentasyllabic word.

    fruor, fruī, frūctus sum + abl., *to enjoy.*

        fruī: with **dā mihi**, *grant it to me to enjoy.*

    pater: i.e., Jupiter.

    Diānae: indirect object with **dedit**, paralleling **Dā mihi** in the preceding clause, but also in a possessive sense with **pater**; Daphne again turns to Diana as a model (cf. 476) in her resistance to Apollo.

488   **obsequor, obsequī, obsecūtus sum**, *to comply, obey.*

    tē . . . vetat (489): the prose order would be **iste decor tē esse vetat quod optās**; for added vividness, the narrator addresses Daphne directly.

    decor, decōris, m., *beauty, grace; elegance, charm.*

        Note the parallelism of **Ille . . . obsequitur . . . decor iste . . . vetat** (489), contrasting her father's compliance with what Daphne's own beauty forbids.

    quod optās: *what you desire.*

489   **esse . . . repugnat**: the line's "special effects" are spectacular; the alliterative juxtaposition of the antithetical **vetat** and **vōtō**, the harsh repetition of **t** (six times), the mournful assonance of long **ō** at the center of the verse, the chiasmus **vōtōque tuō tua fōrma**, and the strong, metaphorical verb **repugnat** at line's end all dramatize the impossibility of the maiden's prayer.

    *__vōtum, -ī__, n., *a vow; prayer, wish.*

    *__fōrma, -ae__, f., *form, shape; beauty.*

    repugnō, -āre, -āvī, -ātūrus, *to offer resistance, fight back; to oppose, be inconsistent with* (+ dat.).

490   **vīsae . . . Daphnēs**: with both **amat** and **cupit cōnūbia**, *as soon as he has seen Daphne, he loves her and desires to marry her.*

    cupit . . . cupit (491): the word is repeated for emphasis, and perhaps as a reminder of Cupid's role (the god's name and the verb **cupere** are, of course, from the same root).

    Daphnēs: gen., whereas in English we might say *marriage with Daphne.*

485   inque patris blandīs haerēns cervīce lacertīs,
      "Dā mihi perpetuā, genitor cārissime," dīxit,
      "virginitāte fruī; dedit hoc pater ante Diānae."
      Ille quidem obsequitur; sed tē decor iste, quod optās,
      esse vetat, vōtōque tuō tua fōrma repugnat.
490   Phoebus amat vīsaeque cupit cōnūbia Daphnēs,
      quodque cupit, spērat, suaque illum ōrācula fallunt.
      Utque levēs stipulae dēmptīs adolentur aristīs,

Discussion Questions

1.   How is the interlocked order of 485 suited to the sense?

2.   Comment on the vignette of Daphne and her father Peneus (481–88); how are his demands typical of any Greek or Roman father, and by what devices does Daphne persuade him to set them aside?

---

491   spērat: with **quod cupit**, *and what he desires he hopes (to achieve)*; cf. spērandō (496).
      ōrāculum, -ī, n., *oracle*; here, *oracular ability*.
      illum ōrācula fallunt: the lilting alliteration adds to the mood; the point here is that a god with Apollo's prophetic powers (**sua** here is especially emphatic) should not be "hoping" for anything, since he ought to know precisely what the future holds.
      *fallō, fallere, fefellī, falsus, *to deceive, trick; to disappoint.*
492   Ut . . . / sīc . . . (495): *just as . . . so . . .*; these words set up the first of two extended similes in the story (cf. Ut . . . / sīc . . . 533–39).
      *levis, -is, -e, *light* (in weight); *nimble; gentle; unsubstantial, thin.*
      stipula, -ae, f., *stalk* (of a grain plant); *stubble* (left in a field once the grain has been harvested), *straw.*
      *dēmō, dēmere, dēmpsī, dēmptus, *to remove, take away; to cut off.*
      adoleō, adolēre, adoluī, adultus, *to burn ritually, cremate; to destroy by fire, burn.*
          adolentur: fields were burnt off to increase their fertility, but the flame that consumes Apollo has an opposite effect (see **sterilem** 496); Ovid intends the reader to think of the verb's association with ritual.
      arista, -ae, f., *grain, kernel.*

493 **facibus**: antecedent of **quās**; cf. **face** (461).

    saepēs, saepis, f., *a hedge.*

    viātor: travelers used torches to light their way at night.

494 **nimis**: with **admōvit**, *too close.*

    sub lūce: sc. **prīmā**, *just before dawn.*

    relīquit: i.e., which he *has left* unextinguished and still smoldering.

495 **in flammās abiit**: *became totally inflamed* (lit., *passed into flames*).

    pectore tōtō: sc. **in.**

496 ***ūrō, ūrere, ussī, ustus**, *to destroy by fire, burn* (here, metaphorically, *with passion*—cf. *Am.* I.1.26 below).

      ūritur . . . nūtrit: the **u/t/r** soundplay that runs through the line underscores the antithesis between these two verbs, the first of which (enjambed and with a strong diaeresis following) connotes destruction and the other sustenance.

    sterilis, -is, -e, *barren, sterile* (here literally and figuratively, as Apollo's love will be unfulfilled and his hoped-for lover forever chaste).

    spērandō: cf. **spērat** (491); Ovid emphasizes again the futility (and, for a god with oracular powers, the folly) of Apollo's hopes.

    nūtriō, -īre, -īvī, -ītus, *to feed at the breast; to support, nourish.*

497 **inōrnātus, -a, -um**, *unadorned, dishevelled.*

      inōrnātōs . . . capillōs: cf. **positōs . . . capillōs** (477); the word order here suggests Daphne's tresses of hair falling all around her neck. The **-ll-** alliteration adds an aptly delicate touch.

  ***collum, -ī**, n., *neck* (here sc. **in**).

  ***pendeō, pendēre, pependī**, *to be suspended, hang; to hang down (upon* or *over).*

      pendēre capillōs: acc. + infin. after **spectat.**

498 ***cōmō, cōmere, cōmpsī, cōmptus**, *to make beautiful, adorn; to dress, arrange, comb.*

      Quid, sī cōmantur: sc. **capillī** as subject; Apollo imagines the nymph as even more beautiful with a proper "hairdo."

    ait: again the speech verb is delayed but should precede the quotation in English translation; cf. 464.

  ***ignis, ignis**, m., *fire.*

499 ***sīdus, sīderis**, n., *a star, planet*; usually pl., *the stars.*

      sīderibus . . . satis (500): the gasping alliteration of **s**, the stunned assonance of **oculōs . . . ōscula** (*Oh . . . oh . . .*), and the rushing dactyls interrupted at line's end by the succession of monosyllables **quae nōn / est**, all suggest Apollo's quickening pulse and his breathlessness at the sight of the nymph's overpowering beauty.

  ***ōsculum, -ī**, n., diminutive of **ōs, ōris**, n., lit., *little mouth*; most commonly *a kiss* or, pl., *lips* (but generally with a kiss in mind!).

    quae: object of **vīdisse**; the infin. phrase is in turn subject of **est**, *which it is not enough (merely) to have seen* (and not, i.e., to have tasted).

500 **digitōsque manūsque / bracchiaque et . . . lacertōs** (501): polysyndeton, used here to "visualize," almost cinematographically, how Apollo shifts his

ut facibus saepēs ārdent, quās forte viātor
vel nimis admōvit vel iam sub lūce relīquit,
495 sīc deus in flammās abiit, sīc pectore tōtō
ūritur, et sterilem spērandō nūtrit amōrem.
Spectat inōrnātōs collō pendēre capillōs,
et "Quid, sī cōmantur?" ait; videt igne micantēs
sīderibus similēs oculōs; videt ōscula, quae nōn
500 est vīdisse satis; laudat digitōsque manūsque

Discussion Questions

1. What is the intended emotional effect of the anaphora in 495?

2. What are the several points of comparison in the extended simile in verses
    492–96. How is the simile appropriate to a description of Apollo as god of
    the sun? How is it appropriate in view of the reference to Cupid in 461?

And as in empty fields the stubble burns,
Or nightly travellers, when day returns,
Their useless torches on dry hedges throw,
That catch the flames, and kindle all the row;
So burns the god, consuming in desire,
And feeding in his breast a fruitless fire.

John Dryden, 1693

gaze from one part of Daphne's body to another, and another, and yet
another. Note too the progression—a variant of the tricolon crescens (cf.
512–13)—from fingertips and hands, to forearms, and on to *her more than
half-bare upper arms* (and then, tantalizingly, to **sī qua latent**); the god's
passion is heating up here, but a further point of this focus on appendages
becomes clear later in the story (cf. **bracchia** 550).

501 ***bracchium, -ī**, n., *the forearm.*
    nūdōs mediā plūs parte: *more than half exposed* (lit., with abl. of degree of difference, *exposed by more than the middle part*), i.e., bare almost to the shoulder.

502 **sī qua latent**: *whatever (charms) lie hidden.*
    *ōcior, ōcior, ōcius, compar. adj., *swifter, more fleeting* (here with adverbial sense).
        ōcior aurā / illa levī (503): interlocked order.
    *aura, -ae, f., *a breath of air, a breeze.*

503 **revocantis**: *as he* (i.e., Apollo) *calls her back* (lit., *of him calling her back*).
    *resistō, resistere, restitī, *to pause in one's journey, halt, stop.*

504 **Nympha . . . manē . . . / nympha, manē** (505): anaphora underscores the god's urgency.
    *precor, precārī, precātus sum, *to pray for, beg*; parenthetically in the 1st pers. sing., *I beseech, pray.*
    Pēnēi: Greek voc. form, *daughter of Peneus* (see on **Pēnēis** 472).
    *īnsequor, īnsequī, īnsecūtus sum, *to pursue, chase.*
    hostis: *as an enemy.*

505 **Sīc**: sc. **Ut mē fugis**, *just as you are fleeing me, so . . .* ; anaphora and asyndeton mark out the series of comparisons.
    agna, -ae, f., *a ewe lamb.*
        agna lupum . . . aquilam . . . columbae (506): chiasmus.
    cerva, -ae, f., *a female deer, doe.*

506 **aquila, -ae**, f., *an eagle.*
    fugiunt trepidante columbae: the clattering dentals and quick dactyls suggest the birds' alarm.
    *trepidō, -āre, -āvī, -ātus, *to panic; to tremble, quiver.*
    *columba, -ae, f., *a pigeon, dove.*

507 ***quisque, quaeque, quidque**, *each* (here, *each creature*; sc. **fugit**).
    amor . . . sequendī: i.e., not an enemy's hostile intent. Note the phrase's parallelism to **sim tibi causa dolōris** (509); Apollo's point is that **amor** should not beget **dolor**.

508 **Mē miserum**: acc. of exclamation.
    nē: with all three jussives, **cadās, notent**, and **sim**.
    *indignus, -a, -um, *unworthy (of), not deserving (to)* + infin.; *innocent.*
        indigna: probably n. acc. pl. with **crūra** (509), though it might, like **prōna**, modify the understood subject of **cadās** (Daphne); the sense is much the same either way.

509 **crūs, crūris**, n., *leg, shin.*
    *notō, -āre, -āvī, -ātus, *to mark, brand; to scar; to notice; to inscribe.*
    sentis, sentis, m., *a thorny bush, bramble, briar.*

510 ***asper, aspera, asperum**, *rough, harsh* (to the touch); *wild, uncultivated.*
    quā, adv., *in which part, where.*
    *properō, -āre, -āvī, -ātus, *to act with haste, be quick; to hurry, rush* (either with a direct object or intransitively).

bracchiaque et nūdōs mediā plūs parte lacertōs;
sīqua latent, meliōra putat.
　　　　　　　　Fugit ōcior aurā
illa levī neque ad haec revocantis verba resistit:
"Nympha, precor, Pēnēi, manē! Nōn īnsequor hostis;
505　nympha, manē! Sīc agna lupum, sīc cerva leōnem,
sīc aquilam pennā fugiunt trepidante columbae,
hostēs quaeque suōs; amor est mihi causa sequendī.
Mē miserum—nē prōna cadās, indignave laedī
crūra notent sentēs, et sim tibi causa dolōris!
510　Aspera, quā properās, loca sunt: moderātius, ōrō,
curre fugamque inhibē; moderātius īnsequar ipse.
Cui placeās, inquīre tamen; nōn incola montis,
nōn ego sum pāstor, nōn hīc armenta gregēsque

Discussion Question

How does the poet's language in 497–502 compel readers to visualize the
scene?

---

　　　　　　properās: the breathless dactyls of 510–11 match Apollo's rapid pace.
　　　*moderātus, -a, -um, *temperate, moderate, restrained*; here, *slow.*
　　　　moderātius . . . moderātius (511): another urgent repetition (cf. manē ·
　　　　　　. . . manē 504–05 and Nescīs . . . nescīs 514), but a humorous one;
　　　　　　Apollo pleads with Daphne, not to stop, but just to slow down, and he
　　　　　　promises (do we believe him?!) that he will do likewise.
511　*fuga, -ae, f., *running away, flight.*
　　　　inhibeō, -ēre, -uī, -itus, *to restrain, hold back.*
512　Cui placeās: subjn. indirect question with inquīre (which in standard prose
　　　　order would precede).
　　　　inquīrō, inquīrere, inquīsīvī, inquīsītus, *to search out, inquire, ask.*
　　　　nōn . . . / nōn . . . nōn (513): anaphora, use of the pronoun subject ego,
　　　　　　and the tricolon crescens all emphasize Apollo's indignation.
513　pāstor, pāstōris, m., *shepherd.*
　　　　armentum, -ī, n., *a herd of cattle.*
　　　　grex, gregis, m., *a herd, a flock (of sheep).*
　　　　　　Apollo was himself god of shepherds, but he does not want this lovely
　　　　　　girl to mistake him for one of them.

514   **horridus, -a, -um**, *having a rough surface; rough, wild, uncouth.*
515   **ideō**, adv., *for that reason, therefore.*
      Mihi . . . servit (516): the pronoun's position adds to the impression of the
      god's arrogance, as does his enumeration of the several shrines at which he
      was worshipped (the last three of them in Asia Minor); polysyndeton and
      the rapid dactylic rhythm add to the effect.
      Delphicus, -a, -um, *Delphic, of Delphi* (a town of Phocis known as site of
      Apollo's oracle—see on **Parnāsī** 467).
      *****tellūs, tellūris**, f., *land, earth.*
516   **Claros, Clarī**, f., *Claros* (an Ionian town sacred to Apollo).
      Tenedos, Tenedī, f., *Tenedos* (an Aegean island off the coast of Troy where
      there was also a temple dedicated to the god).
      Patarēus, -a, -um, *of Patara* (a coastal city in Lycia, site of another oracle
      of Apollo).
      *****rēgia, -ae**, f., *palace, royal house*; here, *a shrine.*
      serviō, -īre, -īvī, -ītūrus + dat., *to serve* (a master), *be the servant of.*
          servit: sing. to agree with the nearest noun in the series, but also because
          all these lands and their shrines are thought of collectively, and
          through personification, as slave to the god's dominion.
517   **Iūppiter, Iovis**, m., *Jupiter* (the Roman sky-god, father of Apollo by
      Latona).
      Iūppiter est genitor: assonance underscores the boast.
      per mē . . . per mē (518): again the pronouns (cf. **mihi** 515), anaphora, and
      polysyndeton punctuate the deity's boast.
518   *****pateō, patēre, patuī**, *to be open; to be visible, revealed.*
      concordō, -āre, -āvī, -ātūrus, *to live in harmony; to be in harmony,*
      harmonize.
      *****carmen, carminis**, n., *a ritual utterance, chant, hymn; a song, poem.*
          concordant carmina: an aptly harmonious assonance.
      nervīs: *with the strings (of a lyre)*; see on **nervus** (455). Apollo was the god
      of music.
519   **Certa . . . nostra est**: sc. **sagitta** from the next clause (and in that clause sc.
      est from here); Apollo was the archer god (cf. **sagittīs** 460).
      Certa . . . nostra . . . nostrā . . . / certior (520): chiasmus emphasizes the
      contrast, as do the enjambement of **certior** (to the same metrical position as
      certa) and the diaeresis following.
520   **in vacuō**: with **pectore**; in prose the relative pronoun would precede.
      *****vacuus, -a, -um**, *empty, hollow; carefree, fancy-free* (cf. *Am.* I.1.26 below);
      + abl., *devoid (of), free (from).*
      vulnera: this wound metaphor sets up the reference to Apollo's association
      with the healing arts in 521–24; Apollo was patron of medicine, but he
      could not heal his own wounds (just as, though a prophet, he could not
      foresee his own future—see 491).
521   **inventum, -ī**, n., *discovery, invention.*
      opifer, opifera, opiferum, *bringing help, aiding*; here an epithet of Apollo,
      bringer of aid.

horridus observō. Nescīs, temerāria, nescīs
515 quem fugiās, ideōque fugis. Mihi Delphica tellūs
et Claros et Tenedos Patarēaque rēgia servit;
Iūppiter est genitor; per mē quod eritque fuitque
estque patet; per mē concordant carmina nervīs.
Certa quidem nostra est, nostrā tamen ūna sagitta
520 certior, in vacuō quae vulnera pectore fēcit.
Inventum medicīna meum est, opiferque per orbem
dīcor, et herbārum subiecta potentia nōbīs;
ei mihi, quod nūllīs amor est sānābilis herbīs,

"Daphne and Apollo," Wilhelm Baur, 1639

---

*orbis, orbis, m., *a disc, any disc-shaped object; wheel; orb* (of the sun or moon); *the world.*
522 ***herba, -ae**, f., *a small plant, herb; grass.*
    herbārum . . . nōbīs: the prose order would be **potentia herbārum nōbīs** (dat. with compounds) **subiecta (est)**.
    subiciō, subicere, subiēcī, subiectus, *to cast upward; to place beneath; to place under the control of.*
*potentia, -ae, f., *power, potency*; here, *healing power.*
523   **ei**, interj. expressing anguish and used commonly with **mihi**, *oh miserable me!*
    nūllīs: set far in advance of **herbīs** for emphasis; the point Apollo makes is in one sense invalid, since Ovid himself had authored a tongue-in-cheek poetry book titled *Remedia Amoris* ("Cures for Love")!
    sānābilis, -is, -e, *curable, remediable.*

524   **nec . . . artēs**: the parallel ABCABCD structure, with the subject **artēs**
       delayed to line's end, effectively closes Apollo's plaint.
       ***prōsum, prōdesse, prōfuī** + dat., irreg., *to be of use to, benefit, help*;
       +infin., *to be beneficial* (to do something).
       quae: the antecedent, **artēs**, follows the relative pronoun, rather than
       preceding it, an arrangement common in verse.
       artēs: i.e., of medicine.
525   **locūtūrum**: sc. **Apollinem** (object of **fūgit**); English would use a clause
       rather than the participial phrase, *as he was about to say more.*
       ***timidus, -a, -um**, *fearful, timorous* (though sometimes applied to situations
       rather than persons, the word here is, strictly speaking, a transferred
       epithet—cf. IV.100 below).
       cursus, -ūs, m., (the act of) *running, flight; course.*
526   **fūgit . . . relīquit**: the line's clipped spondees, elisions, and framing verbs
       underscore the abruptness of Daphne's flight from the god's impassioned
       appeal; **fūgit** here is not just *fled*, but *outdistanced* or (nearly) *escaped.*
       cum . . . ipsō: sc. **deō**.
       imperfectus, -a, -um, *incomplete, unfinished.*
527   **Tum quoque**: i.e., even as she quickened her flight.
       vīsa: sc. **est** (ellipsis—forms of the verb **sum, esse** are frequently omitted in
       Latin prose and verse).
       decēns, decentis, *fitting, appropriate; graceful, attractive.*
       nūdō, -āre, -āvī, -ātus, *to strip, lay bare, expose.*
            nūdābant . . . vibrābant (528) **. . . dabat** (529): the near-rhyming and
            similarly positioned "continuous action" imperfects, each with
            object/subject or subject/object following, provide a sort of motion
            picture of the nymph's flight.
       corpora: pl. for sing., to suggest the parts of her body.
528   **obvius, -a, -um**, *in the way, opposing*; here, *at her face* or *oncoming.*
            obviaque . . . vestēs: with its v/s alliteration the line onomatopoetically
            suggests the whooshing sounds of Daphne's flight through the
            winds—the audio-track, as it were, to Ovid's video (cf. on *Am.* I.2.46
            below).
            obvia . . . capillōs (529): two golden lines (cf. 484), with interlocked
            word order and verbal axial symmetry; the effect here is that we see
            the actions first, before the objects themselves.
       ***adversus, -a, -um**, *opposite (to), facing, turned toward.*
       vibrō, -āre, -āvī, -ātus, *to wave, (cause to) flutter.*
       flāmen, flāminis, n., *a blast, gust (of wind); wind, breeze.*
529   **et levis . . . capillōs**: another highly musical verse, with alliteration of the
       sibilant s, the l/r liquids, and the assonant **-ōs/-ō/-ōs**, sounding almost like
       the shrieking of the wind as its breezes course round the nymph's body.
       levis: not *gentle* here, but *quick, fleeting.*
       ***impellō, impellere, impulī, impulsus**, *to strike, beat against; to motivate.*
            impulsōs . . . capillōs: Latin often uses a participle where English would
            use a finite verb; with **retrō dabat**, translate *struck against her hair*

nec prōsunt dominō, quae prōsunt omnibus, artēs!"
525   Plūra locūtūrum timidō Pēnēia cursū
fūgit, cumque ipsō verba imperfecta relīquit.
Tum quoque vīsa decēns: nūdābant corpora ventī,
obviaque adversās vibrābant flāmina vestēs,
et levis impulsōs retrō dabat aura capillōs,
530   auctaque fōrma fugā est. Sed enim nōn sustinet ultrā
perdere blanditiās iuvenis deus, utque monēbat

Discussion Questions

1.   In lines 504–24, Apollo argues a number of different points in his effort to
     persuade Daphne to stop fleeing. What are his principal arguments and how
     do they reflect upon his character? Is this characterization consistent with his
     behavior in the story's opening scene?

2.   Remembering that Apollo is racing madly after Daphne as he delivers the
     speech in 504–24, would you say that the overall effect of the scene is
     serious or comic? How does the content of the speech support your view?

---

          and sent it streaming behind her.
     *retrō, adv., *toward the rear, backwards, behind.*
530   **enim**: with **sed**, *but in fact*; i.e., despite Daphne's growing attractiveness,
     Apollo intends no more imploring speeches (like the one in 504–24) but
     will quicken his pursuit.
     *sustineō, sustinēre, sustinuī, *to hold up, support; to sustain;* + infin., *to be
     able* (to do something) *without relenting.*
     ultrā, adv., *on the far side, beyond; further, any longer.*
531   ***perdō, perdere, perdidī, perditus**, *to destroy, ruin; to waste.*
     *blanditia, -ae, f., often pl. with sing. meaning, *flattery, alluring speech.*
     monēbat: some manuscripts have **movēbat**, *was stirring* (for the idea cf.
     amor est mihi causa sequendī), but **Amor** here, with the intensive **ipse**,
     likely refers to Cupid himself (cf. 480) and **monēbat** is the livelier reading.

532   **admittō, admittere, admīsī, admissus**, *to admit, receive; to give rein to, direct*.

       admissō . . . passū: *with quickened pace*.

    *****passus, -ūs**, m., *step, pace, stride*.

533   **Ut . . . cum . . . / sīc . . .** (539): *just as when . . . so . . .*; another extended simile (cf. 492–96).

     canis . . . arvō: the interlocked order produces a neat word-picture with the rabbit actually situated in the middle of the desolate field and "trapped," so to speak, by the **canis . . . Gallicus**; Horace in one of his *Odes* similarly compares Cleopatra, in her flight from Octavian after Actium, to a hunted rabbit.

     Gallicus, -a, -um, *Gallic, of Gaul* (a region of Europe north of Italy noted for its hunting dogs).

    *****arvum, -ī**, n., *field*.

534   **hic praedam . . . petit, ille salūtem**: note the ABCAB arrangement (which is replicated in 539), the quick dactyls, and the harsh **d/t/p** alliteration; take **pedibus petit** with both subjects (**hic**, the hound, and **ille**, the hare) and with both objects.

    *****praeda, -ae**, f., *booty, plunder; prey, game*.

     salūs, salūtis, f., *safety, well-being*.

535   **alter . . . / alter** (537): the two couplets are neatly balanced, with the hound hoping to catch hold of its prey and snapping at it with its mouth, and the rabbit uncertain whether or not it has already been caught and ripping itself free from the hound's jaws.

     inhaereō, inhaerēre, inhaesī, inhaesūrus, *to be attached to, stick to*; (of an animal) *to hold on (to) with its teeth*.

       inhaesūrō similis: *like an animal about to grab its prey with its teeth*.

     iam iamque: anaphora; this adv. is commonly repeated for emotional emphasis.

536   **spērat . . . rostrō**: the verse is highly alliterative, and the series of harsh dentals (eight **t**'s) and the snarling **r**'s and **s**'s may be deliberately onomatopoetic.

     extentō . . . rostrō: the parallelism with **admissō . . . passū** (532) reinforces the simile; here, with the wide separation of participle and noun, the phrase is stretched out across the verse, just as the dog's snout is extended in the direction of its prey—possibly an effect intended by Ovid.

    *****stringō, stringere, strīnxī, strictus**, *to bind, secure; to draw tight; to draw close to, touch*.

     rostrum, -ī, n., *snout, muzzle*.

537   **ambiguum, -ī**, n., *ambiguity*; **in ambiguō**, idiom, *in a state of uncertainty, uncertain*.

    *****an**, conj., often introducing indirect questions, *whether, or, if*.

     comprēndō, comprēndere, comprēndī, comprēnsus, *to seize, catch*.

538   *****morsus, -ūs**, m., *bite* (of an animal); pl., by metonymy, *teeth, jaws*.

     ēripitur: passive but with a reflexive sense (a usage comparable to the Greek middle voice and common in Latin poetry), *rips itself from*.

ipse Amor, admissō sequitur vestīgia passū.
Ut canis in vacuō leporem cum Gallicus arvō
vīdit, et hic praedam pedibus petit, ille salūtem—
535 alter inhaesūrō similis iam iamque tenēre
spērat, et extentō stringit vestīgia rostrō;
alter in ambiguō est an sit comprēnsus, et ipsīs
morsibus ēripitur, tangentiaque ōra relinquit—
sīc deus et virgō; est hic spē celer, illa timōre.
540 Quī tamen īnsequitur, pennīs adiūtus Amōris,
ōcior est, requiemque negat, tergōque fugācis

Discussion Question

Compare the simile in 533–39 with those at 492–96 and 505–07; in what
respects are they alike and in what respects different? Which is more
sympathetic to Apollo? How does Ovid's comparison of Daphne with a
hunted animal relate to his depiction of her earlier in the story?

---

*tangō, tangere, tetigī, tāctus, *to touch*.
relinquit: here, *escapes from*.
539 **hic spē celer, illa timōre**: **celer** belongs with both phrases, just as **pedibus
petit** connects **hic praedam** and **ille salūtem** in 534; the repetition of
structure and diction between that line and this helps make the equation,
while the two couplets intervening describe first the **hic** (535–36), then the
ille (537–38).
*spēs, speī, f., *hope*.
540 **Quī**: sc. the antecedent **is** (i.e., Apollo) from **ōcior est** (541).
Amōris: with **pennīs adiūtus** we are again meant to think not only of love
but of Cupid, who is controlling the action behind the scenes.
541 **requiēs, requiētis**, acc. usually **requiem**, f., *rest, respite*.
*negō, -āre, -āvī, -ātus, *to say (that) not; to refuse, deny*.
tergō: dat. with **imminet**.
fugāx, fugācis, *evasive, fugitive* (used here as a noun).

542   immineō, imminēre, *to rise up, overhang; to press closely (upon); to threaten.*
    *crīnis, crīnis, m., *a lock of hair*; pl. or collective sing., *hair.*
    *spargō, spargere, sparsī, sparsus, *to scatter, strew; to allow to stream out.*
    cervīcibus: sc. in; here, as often with this word, pl. form with sing. meaning.
    afflō, -āre, -āvī, -ātus, *to breathe on, blow on.*
543   *absūmō, absūmere, absūmpsī, absūmptus, *to use up; to wear out, exhaust.*
    *expallēscō, expallēscere, expalluī, *to grow pale.*
        expalluit illa: the alliterative -ll- lends a delicate, perhaps even pathetic effect.
    *citus, -a, -um, *swift, rapid.*
545   *ops, opis, f., *power, ability; resources; aid.*
    *flūmen, flūminis, n., *stream, river.*
        flūmina . . . habētis: Daphne addresses the river's streams as the very spirit of her father, *if you streams have . . .*; note the internal rhyme in flūmina nūmen ha-.
    *nūmen, nūminis, n., *a nod* (of assent); *divine power, supernatural influence.*
547   Quā: again the antecedent (figūram) follows.
        There are interpolations and other corruptions in the manuscripts at this point in the text; the best solution seems to be to omit verse 546.
    *nimium, adv., *too much, excessively.*
    *mūtō, -āre, -āvī, -ātus, *to exchange; to change, replace; to transform.*
    *figūra, -ae, f., *form, composition; outward appearance.*
548   prex, precis, f., *entreaty, prayer.*
    torpor, torpōris, m., *numbness, paralysis.*
    *artus, -ūs, m., *a joint of the body; arm, leg, limb.*
549   *mollis, -is, -e, *soft, tender; gentle.*
        mollia . . . librō: the line's interlocked order neatly suits its meaning.
    *cingō, cingere, cīnxī, cīnctus, *to surround, encircle.*
    *tenuis, -is, -e, *slender, thin.*
    praecordia, -ōrum, n. pl., *the chest, breast.*
    liber, librī, m., *the inner bark of a tree* (cf. cortice 554); *a book.*
550   *frōns, frondis, f., *the leafy part of a tree, foliage.*
    *crēscō, crēscere, crēvī, crētūrus, *to be born, arise; to increase, change into* (by growing); *to grow, bud.*
551   pēs . . . vēlōx pigrīs rādīcibus: chiasmus.
    vēlōx, vēlōcis, *rapid, swift.*
    piger, pigra, pigrum, *sluggish, inactive; motionless, inert.*
    *rādīx, rādīcis, f., *root* (of a plant or tree).
552   ōra cacūmen habet: Ovid's cinematographic eye moves quickly from foot to head in 551-52; the image here is elaborated in 567.
    *cacūmen, cacūminis, n., *peak, top* (especially of an object that tapers upward to a point); here, *treetop.*
    remaneō, remanēre, remānsī, remansūrus, *to remain; to persist, endure.*
        remanet nitor: i.e., in the sheen of the tree's leaves.

imminet, et crīnem sparsum cervīcibus afflat.
Vīribus absūmptīs, expalluit illa, citaeque
victa labōre fugae, spectāns Pēnēidas undās,
545 "Fer, pater," inquit, "opem, sī flūmina nūmen habētis!
547 Quā nimium placuī, mūtandō perde figūram!"
Vix prece fīnītā, torpor gravis occupat artūs;
mollia cinguntur tenuī praecordia librō,
550 in frondem crīnēs, in rāmōs bracchia crēscunt;
pēs modo tam vēlōx pigrīs rādīcibus haeret,
ōra cacūmen habet; remanet nitor ūnus in illā.
      Hanc quoque Phoebus amat, positāque in stīpite dextrā
sentit adhūc trepidāre novō sub cortice pectus,

Discussion Questions

1. What is the effect of the polysyndeton in 541–42?

2. What is the purpose of the chiasmus in 551?

3. It has been said that meter is to a poem what the soundtrack is to a film. How does Ovid's manipulation of the meter in 548–52 enliven the images he describes? Think specifically of the alternation of dactyls and spondees in 549; how does this suit the action of 548–49? Comment on the striking metrical differences between 550 and 552; and what is the effect of the shift after the first foot in 551?

4. How is the meter in 553–54 appropriate to the action described?

---

nitor, nitōris, m., *brightness, splendor; beauty.*
553 **Hanc:** the shift from **illā** (552) to **hanc** shows the transformation is complete.
stīpes, stīpitis, m., *the trunk of a tree.*
554 **trepidāre . . . pectus:** acc. + infin. after **sentit.**
novō sub cortice: there is perhaps a deliberate oxymoron in the description
  of something that is old and tough with an epithet meaning *fresh and new.*
cortex, corticis, m., *the tough outer bark of a tree.*
pectus: here, *her heart.*

555   **complector, complectī, complexus sum**, *to hold in the arms, embrace, hug.*
    ***membrum, -ī**, n., *a part of the body, limb, member.*
556   **ōscula dat . . . refugit . . . ōscula**: chiasmus.
    ***lignum, -ī**, n., *firewood; wood; a stump; a shaft.*
    refugiō, refugere, refūgī, refugitus, *to flee, run away; to recoil from.*
557   ***coniūnx, coniugis**, m. or f., *a spouse* (husband or wife).
558   **mea**: repeated from 557 and suspensefully delayed to add emphasis (along
        with **certē** and **semper**) to Apollo's pronouncement.
    habēbunt: in a dual sense, *will possess* and *will display*; Apollo cannot
        actually have the nymph herself, but his hair and his various accoutrements
        will ever be adorned with the leaves and wood of the tree into which she
        has been transformed.
559   ***coma, -ae**, f., *hair.*
    nostrae: with **coma** and **citharae** as well as **pharetrae**.
    ***laurus, -ī**, f., *a laurel tree, bay; a sprig or branch of laurel; a garland of*
    laurel (as a ritual object, especially one sacred to Apollo, or a sign of
    victory).
        laure: in applying this name to the tree, Apollo thus identifies his
        "invention." She who was the nymph **Daphne**, and whose name was
        the Greek word for the laurel tree, has become now **laurus**, with its
        new Latin name, a laurel tree only, subject not only to the control of
        Apollo but even, as the following lines imply, to the triumphant *lords*
        of Latium (**ducibus Latiīs** 560).
560   ***dux, ducis**, m., *leader; commander, general.*
        ducibus Latiīs: dat. with the compound verb **aderis**; Ovid Romanizes
        his story by having Apollo foresee the Roman empire and the
        triumphal processions in which Roman generals wore laurel garlands in
        their hair when celebrating their military victories.
    Latius, -a, -um, *of Latium, Latin.*
    ***triumphus, -ī**, m., *the ritual shout "triumphe"* (cf. *Am.* I.2.25, 34 below); *a*
    triumph (the ritual procession of a victorious general through the streets of
    Rome); *a victory celebration; a victory.*
        triumphum / vox canet et vīsent . . . Capitōlia pompās (561): an
        elaborate and sonorous chiasmus, appropriate to the ritual train
        described.
561   ***canō, canere, cecinī, cantus**, *to sing, chant; to sing about, celebrate.*
    vīsō, vīsere, vīsī, *to look at, view.*
    Capitōlium, -ī, n., *the Capitoline Hill* (site in Rome of the temple of Jupiter
    Capitolinus, where triumphal processions generally concluded).
        Capitōlia: the pl. form of this noun is often used for the sing. in Latin
        verse, but here, along with **pompās**, Ovid may intend to suggest a
        great series of triumphs over the generations, all of which Apollo can
        foresee because of his prophetic powers (one might compare the
        prophecies of Jupiter to Venus in *Aeneid* I and Anchises to Aeneas in
        Aeneid VI).
    ***pompa, -ae**, f., *a ceremonial procession.*

555   complexusque suīs rāmōs, ut membra, lacertīs
        ōscula dat lignō; refugit tamen ōscula lignum.
        Cui deus "At quoniam coniūnx mea nōn potes esse,
        arbor eris certē" dīxit, "mea! Semper habēbunt
        tē coma, tē citharae, tē nostrae, laure, pharetrae.
560   Tū ducibus Latiīs aderis, cum laeta triumphum
        vōx canet et vīsent longās Capitōlia pompās.
        Postibus Augustīs eadem fīdissima custōs
        ante forēs stābis, mediamque tuēbere quercum,

Discussion Questions

1.   How does the word order in 555 suit the action described?

2.   What is the emotional effect of the anaphora in 559?

3.   What are the purposes of the "Romanizing" elements in 560–63? How would Ovid's audience respond to them? How are the specific Roman elements Ovid has chosen appropriate to the story itself and to the ultimate outcome of Apollo's pursuit of Daphne?

562   **Postibus Augustīs**: dat. with **fīdissima custōs** (and a further Romanization), *most loyal guardian of the Augustan gates*; the entrance to Augustus' imperial palace was adorned with laurel, a symbol of victory and of the emperor's special reverence for Apollo.
        Augustus, -a, -um, *of Augustus; imperial.*
        eadem: here, *ever the same, immutable.*
        *****fīdus, -a, -um**, *faithful, loyal, devoted.*
563   *****foris, foris**, f., *door, entrance* (of a building or room); pl., *double-doors.*
        *****tueor, tuērī, tuitus sum**, *to look at, observe; to watch over, protect* (**tuēbere** = **tuēberis**).
        mediam: *in the middle*, i.e., hanging suspended over the middle of the palace's entranceway.
        quercus, -ūs, f., *an oak tree*; here, *an oak garland* (the **corōna cīvica**, an oak garland traditionally awarded by the Roman government for acts of heroism, also adorned the door to Augustus' palace).

564 **meum . . . capillīs**: interlocked word order.

intōnsus, -a, -um, *uncut, unshorn* (usually of the hair or beard, but also of the foliage of trees).

    intōnsīs . . . capillīs: descriptive abl.; long hair was a mark of youth, and Apollo, of course, was perpetually young.

iuvenālis, -is, -e, *youthful*.

565 **perpetuōs**: *everlasting*, because the laurel tree is evergreen.

honor, honōris, m., *high esteem, honor; a mark of grace, beauty* (here pl. for sing. with **frondis**, *the loveliness of your foliage*).

566 **Fīnierat**: i.e., **fīnīverat** (see on **petiēre** 478); the short clause effectively punctuates Apollo's lengthy prophecy.

Paeān, Paeānis, m., *Paean* (an epithet of Apollo in his aspect as god of healing).

Factīs modo . . . rāmīs: abl. of means, *with her recently created branches*.

laureus, -a, -um, *of laurel, laurel*; here a substantive, *the laurel tree*.

567 **adnuō, adnuere, adnuī, adnūtus**, *to beckon, nod* (the verb means sometimes, but not always, *to nod assent*).

    adnuit . . . cacūmen: with its fluttering alliteration of the hard **d/t/q/c/g** consonants and the sibilant **s**'s, the line provides a sonorous, even onomatopoetic closure to Ovid's tale.

ut caput: *as though it were her head*; for the image cf. 552.

agitō, -āre, -āvī, -ātus, *to move, shake, stir* (**agitāsse** = **agitāvisse**, see on **petiēre** 478).

"Apollo and Daphne"
Antonio Pollaiuolo, ca. 1475
National Gallery, London

utque meum intōnsīs caput est iuvenāle capillīs,
565   tu quoque perpetuōs semper gere frondis honōrēs!"
Fīnierat Paeān; factīs modo laurea rāmīs
adnuit, utque caput vīsa est agitāsse cacūmen.

Discussion Questions

1.   What is the point of addressing Apollo in 566 as "Paean"?

2.   What is your response to the story's outcome and Daphne's fate? Would a Roman's response be the same? Is there any ambiguity (compare the closing scene of the *Aeneid*)?

3.   What further insights might a feminist analysis of this tale provide?

Daphne

"Daphne"
Renée Sintenis, 1930
Museum of Modern Art
New York

Poet, Singer, Necromancer—
I cease to run. I halt you here,
Pursuer, with an answer:

Do what you will.
The blood you've set to music I
Can change to chlorophyll,

And root myself, and with my toes
Wind to subterranean streams.
Through solid rock my strength now grows.

Such now am I, I cease to eat,
But feed on flashes from your eyes;
Light, to my new cells, is meat.

Find then, when you seize my arm
That xylem thickens in my skin
And there are splinters in my charm.

I may give in; I do not lose.
Your hot stare cannot stop my shivering,
With delight, if I so choose.

A.E. Stallings

PYRAMUS AND THISBE

Metamorphoses IV.55–166

This second selection from the *Metamorphoses* is quite unlike the first. The story of Daphne and Apollo was one of unreciprocated love, of power and violence, of male (and divine) aggression, and feminist resistance, told in variously epic and comic tones, and, though set in a primordial epoch, resonating in its final scene with the Roman world of imperialism and Augustan order. Ovid's tale of Pyramus and Thisbe comes in Book IV of the *Metamorphoses*, much later in his cosmic scheme; civilization has advanced from its emergent state in Book I; we are now in the exotic, mystical world of the East, in the Babylon of Queen Semiramis.

And although the unhappy circumstances of our hero and heroine are reminiscent of the frustrated lovers of Roman comedy, as well as of elegy (with its *amātōrēs exclūsī* and its secret encounters), and while Ovid's drama certainly does have some lighter moments, the action is ultimately not comic at all, but unexpectedly tragic. Pyramus and Thisbe have many admirable and heroic traits (Thisbe in particular is strikingly courageous and perceptive—like Daphne in certain respects), but their story lacks the divine action and heroic conflict of epic and the ambiguous political associations with Roman empire and emperor of the poet's Daphne tale; it is instead a purely human and private drama, a sentimental story of youthful romance that comes to a dark and bloody conclusion. In a reversal of the point made at the outset of "Daphne and Apollo," the crisis here is created, not by "the savage wrath of Cupid," but by "blind chance," the impetuousness of two innocent young lovers, and the stern prohibitions of their doubtless well-intended but overly protective parents.

We have no literary sources for this story earlier than Ovid, who describes it as "a little-known tale" (*vulgāris fābula nōn est, Met.* IV.53). Because of its Babylonian setting and the fact that there were rivers named "Pyramus" and "Thisbe" in Cilicia and elsewhere in the eastern Mediterranean, the tale is generally supposed to have originated in the East. Like many of Ovid's episodes, this one is presented as a tale within a tale (hence the quotation marks enclosing the entire Latin text that follows), the first of three love stories narrated in the first half of *Metamorphoses* IV by the three daughters of Minyas, king of Orchomenos in Boeotia. While their fellow townspeople are celebrating a festival in honor of Bacchus, the Minyades, ignoring the example of the Theban king Pentheus (whose destruction for a similar impiety had just been recounted at the end of Book III), reject the god's divinity and remain at home, spinning wool and exchanging stories to pass the time. Of their three amatory tales, only this first one tells of an untainted love—the "ideal" Ovidian love, as Brooks Otis has remarked and as we can see both from the progress of the narrative itself and from the sympathetic comments interjected along the way by Ovid's own "partisan narrator" (as distinguished by Otis from the vile daughter of Minyas who tells the tale and who, in effect, deliberately contrives its unhappy ending). When all three of the tales were concluded, Bacchus' spirit descended on the palace, causing grapevines and ivy to grow out of the sisters' tapestries and looms, and transforming the Minyades themselves into hideous bats.

The tale may be summarized as follows: Pyramus, a handsome Babylonian youth, and his beautiful young neighbor Thisbe (we should imagine them in their teens) fall in love, but are forbidden by their parents to marry or even to meet. At first they communicate only by whispering through a crack discovered in the wall connecting their two houses; like the elegiac lover who reproaches the door that keeps him from his mistress, both Pyramus and Thisbe often scold their wall as though it were alive, but then thank it for the passage it has given to their speech. Eventually, however, longing to share more than just words, the two conspire to leave their homes by night and to meet under a mulberry tree—a tree whose berries were in those days white—near the tomb of king Ninus on the outskirts of the city. Arriving first, Thisbe sees a lioness, drenched with blood from a recent kill and drinking from the nearby stream; she rushes to take refuge in a dark cavern and, in her flight, drops her veil, which the lioness soon finds, shreds with her bloody maw, and then leaves behind. When Pyramus arrives, he sees the animal's tracks and Thisbe's mutilated, blood-stained garment, and mistakenly concludes the worst; blaming himself and rushing to the tree where the two had planned to rendezvous, the youth first kisses Thisbe's veil, then plunges his sword into his groin, spattering the tree's berries and soaking its roots with his blood as he lay dying. Soon Thisbe emerges from the cave, still fearful but determined to see her beloved. When she discovers his body instead and realizes what has happened, she tries at first to arouse him, but then, failing in that, commits suicide with Pyramus' own sword. But before plunging the sword into her breast, Thisbe utters two final prayers, first to their parents, that they allow the cremated remains of both lovers to rest in a single urn, and then to the mulberry tree where they had made their fatal rendezvous, that its own "offspring," its berries, should be forever altered from white to the dark-red hue of blood, to serve both as the tree's own cloak of mourning and as a perpetual reminder of the lovers' suicides. In the story's closing lines we see both of Thisbe's prayers realized—one fulfilling the myth's etiological function (explaining the origin of the purplish-red mulberry), the other bringing the folktale's plot to closure by joining the two lovers at last in death as their parents had forbidden them in life.

With its implicit warnings for young people who may exercise too little control over their passions, and for parents who try to exercise too much, Ovid's story is a folktale rather than a myth in the usual Greco-Roman sense, one that quickly transcends its eastern setting and assumes, as the poet intended, a universal quality that has insured its appeal to subsequent generations. One of Ovid's most beautiful tales of love, and beautifully told, "Pyramus and Thisbe" has inspired countless imitations and adaptations over the centuries. An early version appears in the *Fabulae* of the 2nd-century A.D. mythographer Hyginus. Dante alludes to the tale, which is retold later in the 14th century by both Boccaccio and Chaucer (in his "Legende of Goode Women") and which provides the subject of several plays, both comic and tragic, the best known of them the burlesque play-within-a-play performed by the "mechanicals" in Shakespeare's *Midsummer Night's Dream* (and of course *Romeo and Juliet* takes up the themes of parental restriction and the suicide of young lovers). Other poets have been captivated by the tale, among them John Donne in an epigram composed in 1631, the year of his death. Countless representations have appeared in the visual arts as well, including paintings, woodcuts, and engravings, among them a series of drawings by both Rubens and Rembrandt from the 17th century and even, from the same period, an etching by Stefano Della Bella for a set of playing cards. We have besides, from the 18th into the 20th century, several cantatas, more than half a dozen ballets, and about 20 operas, including Federico Ghisi's *Piramo e Tisbe*, composed in the 1940's and based upon Shakespeare's adaptation.

Like so many others over the centuries who have treasured the story of "Pyramus and Thisbe," modern readers of Ovid's original will appreciate the easy, dynamic flow of his narrative, the brilliant effects of sound and sight (not least the poet's manipulation of dark/light imagery and sexual metaphor), and especially the humanity of his star-crossed hero and heroine, the tenderness of their love, the depth of their courage, and the intensity of passion that compels both, inexorably, to the act of suicide.

At every tyme whan they durste soo,
Upon the o syde of the walle stood he,
And on that other syde stood Tesbe,
The swoote soune of other to receyve.

Chaucer, Legende of Goode Women, lines 749-52

"Thisbe," J. W. Waterhouse, 1909

55   ***Pȳramus, -ī, m.**, *Pyramus* (a Babylonian youth).
    *Thisbē, Thisbēs, f., *Thisbe* (a Babylonian maiden, Pyramus' neighbor and inamorata; for the Greek case endings, see on **Daphnē** *Met.* I.452).
    iuvenum pulcherrimus alter, / altera . . . praelāta puellīs (56): chiasmus; the entire phrase is in apposition to **Pȳramus et Thisbē**, the subjects of **tenuēre** (57).

56   **quās**: the antecedent is **puellīs**.
    oriēns, orientis, m., *the rising sun, dawn; the eastern world, the orient.*
    praelāta: with **altera**; here, *preferred.*

57   **contiguus, -a, -um**, *adjacent, connected.*
    tenuēre: = **tenuērunt**, *had* or *occupied.*
    ubi . . . urbem (58): an epic periphrasis for the ancient city of Babylon; positioning of the adjective/noun pair **altam / . . . urbem** at the ends of the verses adds to the epic effect.

58   **coctilis, -is, -e**, *baked; made of fired bricks.*
    mūrīs: the vast walls and gardens of Babylon were among the wonders of the ancient world.
    Semīramis, Semīramidis, f., *Semiramis* (legendary queen of Assyria, wife of Ninus, and founder of Babylon).

59   **nōtitia, -ae, f.**, *acquaintance.*
    Nōtitiam prīmōsque gradūs: sc. **amōris**, *their acquaintance and the first steps (of their love)*; or possibly a hendiadys, *the first stage of their acquaintance.*
    gradus, -ūs, m., *step, pace; phase, stage* (in a process).
    vīcīnia, -ae, f., *nearby area, vicinity; nearness, proximity.*

60   **Taedae . . . iūre**: *in the bond of marriage* (metonymy— lit., *with the sanction of the [wedding] torch*).
    *iūs, iūris, n., *law, legal sanction; legal authority, right.*
    *coeō, coīre, coiī, coitus, *to come together, meet; to form an alliance* (here, *of marriage*).
    coīssent: potential subjn., *they would have come together.*

61   **vetuēre patrēs . . . potuēre vetāre**: understand **patrēs** with **potuēre**, and note the sound-play and chiastic arrangement.
    quod: the entire clause in 62 is the antecedent (*but—what they could not prevent—they both burned . . .*).

62   **aequus, -a, -um**, *level, even*; **ex aequō**, idiom, *at the same level, equally.*
  *mēns, mentis, f., *the mind.*

63   **cōnscius, -ī, m.**, *accomplice, witness.*
    abest . . . aestuat (64): here and often throughout the story (cf. 84–92) Ovid lapses into the historical present to engage the reader and add vividness to his narrative.
    nūtus, -ūs, m., *a nod of the head* (especially a nod of assent).

64   **quōque**: i.e., **quō** + **que**; **quō . . . magis . . . (eō) magis**, *the more . . . the more.*
    magis tegitur, tēctus magis: chiasmus.

55   "Pȳramus et Thisbē, iuvenum pulcherrimus alter,
altera, quās oriēns habuit, praelāta puellīs,
contiguās tenuēre domōs, ubi dīcitur altam
coctilibus mūrīs cīnxisse Semīramis urbem.
Nōtitiam prīmōsque gradūs vīcīnia fēcit;
60 tempore crēvit amor. Taedae quoque iūre coīssent,
sed vetuēre patrēs; quod nōn potuēre vetāre,
ex aequō captīs ardēbant mentibus ambō.
Cōnscius omnis abest, nūtū signīsque loquuntur,
quōque magis tegitur, tēctus magis aestuat ignis.
65   "Fissus erat tenuī rīmā, quam dūxerat ōlim,
cum fieret, pariēs domuī commūnis utrīque.
Id vitium nūllī per saecula longa notātum—

Discussion Questions

1. How is the chiasmus in 55–56 appropriate to the description of Pyramus and Thisbe and the houses in which they lived?

2. How is the symmetry of 62 appropriate to the circumstance described? And what may the series of spondees and hard consonants be intended to suggest?

3. Comment on the metaphor in 62–64. How is the image enhanced through the anaphora and word order in 64?

4. Explain the aptness of the interlocked word order in 66.

---

 *tegō, tegere, tēxī, tēctus, *to cover; to hide, conceal.*
 aestuō, -āre, -āvī, -ātus, *to burn fiercely, blaze; to burn with desire.*
 ignis: subject of both **tegitur** and **aestuat.**
65 findō, findere, fidī, fissus, *to split apart; to open up.*
 dūxerat: *it had developed;* **pariēs . . . commūnis** is subject of all three verbs in the sentence.
66 *pariēs, parietis, m., *wall.*
 domuī . . . utrīque: dat. with **commūnis.**
67 *vitium, -ī, n., *defect, fault; flaw, imperfection; vice.*
 nūllī: dat. with **notātum,** *known to nobody.*
 saeculum, -ī, n., *generation, age* (i.e., a long period of time).

68   **quid . . . amor**: the question, out of the narrator's own sense of excitement, anticipates the discovery in **prīmī vīdistīs amantēs**.
    prīmī: as often in Latin, the adj. has adverbial force (cf. **tūtae** 69).
    amantēs: the participle of **amō** often functions as a noun, *lovers* (cf. 73, 108, and *Am.* I.9.25 below).

69   **iter facere**, idiom, *to clear a way, grant passage*; with **vocis**, *to create a pathway to speech*, a personification elaborated in **tūtae . . . blanditiae . . . trānsīre solēbant** (70).
    *****tūtus, -a, -um**, *safe, secure*.
        tūtae . . . minimō (70): interlocked order.
    illud: i.e., **iter**.

71   *****hinc**, adv., *from this place; from* or *on this side*.
    illinc, adv., *from that place; from* or *on that side*.
    hinc Thisbē, Pȳramus illinc: the chiastic arrangement brings the two lovers together, but the strong diaeresis (like the wall) keeps them apart—more marvelous Ovidian wordplay!

72   **in vicēs**, idiomatic adv., *(each) in turn, alternately*.
    fuerat captātus: = **captātus erat**; not just *had been felt* or *listened for*, but far more passionately, *had been seized at and inhaled*—the lovers' lips cannot quite touch (see lines 75, 79–80), but each frantically gasps in the other's breath through the tiny crack.
    anhēlitus, -ūs, m., *gasping, panting; breath, breathing*.

73   **invidus, -a, -um**, *malevolent, hateful; envious, jealous* (the door itself has become an enemy!).
    quid, here an adv., *why?*
    *****obstō, obstāre, obstitī, obstātūrus** + dat., *to face; to stand in the way (of), obstruct*.

74   **Quantum erat**: **esset**, a potential subjunctive, might be expected; the construction takes a result clause, *How great a matter would it be to . . . ?* Diaeresis punctuates the query.
    tōtō nōs corpore iungī: the lovers' desire is made explicit, and the ō/ō/ō assonance perhaps onomatopoetically mimics their cries of longing.

75   **vel**: here, *at least*.
    ad ōscula danda: a gerundive phrase expressing purpose; freely, *for us to kiss*.

76   **ingrātus, -a, -um**, *ungrateful, thankless, unappreciative*.
    *****fateor, fatērī, fassus sum**, *to acknowledge, admit, confess*.

77   **quod**: here, *the fact that*; the entire **quod** clause is object of **dēbēre** (76).
    *****amīcus, -a, -um**, *friendly, loving; of a friend* or *lover*.
    trānsitus, -ūs, m., *passage, path*.
        The noun here looks back to **trānsīre** (70) and continues the personification of 69–70; the line's repeated sibilants (s six times) suggest the sounds of the lovers' whispering.
    *****auris, auris**, f., *the ear*.

78   **Tālia**: object of **locūtī**.
    *****nēquīquam**, adv., *with no effect, to no avail, in vain*.

quid nōn sentit amor?—prīmī vīdistis amantēs,
et vōcis fēcistis iter; tūtaeque per illud
70   murmure blanditiae minimō trānsīre solēbant.
Saepe, ubi cōnstiterant hinc Thisbē, Pȳramus illinc,
inque vicēs fuerat captātus anhēlitus ōris,
'Invide,' dīcēbant, 'pariēs, quid amantibus obstās?
Quantum erat, ut sinerēs tōtō nōs corpore iungī
75   aut, hoc sī nimium est, vel ad ōscula danda patērēs?
Nec sumus ingrātī: tibi nōs dēbēre fatēmur,
quod datus est verbīs ad amīcās trānsitus aurēs.'
Tālia dīversā nēquīquam sēde locūtī,
sub noctem dīxēre, 'Valē,' partīque dedēre

Discussion Questions

1.   Why does the narrator suddenly shift to the use of second person verbs in 68–69? What is the effect?

2.   Why is the personification in 69–70 especially appropriate in this context?

3.   What is the effect of the **m/n** alliteration in 70?

4.   How does the imaginative view of the inanimate world expressed by the two lovers in 73–77 coincide with the poet's own fantasizing images? In light of the overarching imagery of the *Metamorphoses* (think, for example, of Daphne's transformation into a tree that can hear and communicate), how is it perfectly "logical" that Pyramus and Thisbe should "often" (**saepe** 71) address the wall shared by their two houses? Once you understand how Ovid "animates" the inanimate world, what seems to be the best translation of **amīcās . . . aurēs** (77)?

5.   How again in verse 78 is the word order a perfect construct for the situation described?

---

*sēdēs, sēdis, f., *seat; home; place, position* (here, sc. ē).
79   sub: here, *just before.*
    dīxēre . . . dedēre: = dīxērunt . . . dedērunt; the subject quisque (80) often takes a pl. verb, *they each.*
    partī . . . suae (80): *their own side (of the wall)*; the interlocked order (partī . . . / ōscula . . . suae . . . nōn pervenientia) matches the complications of their kissing!

80 **nōn pervenientia**: English would use a relative clause, *that did not come through.*

contrā: here adv., *on the opposite side.*

81 **Postera . . . ignēs**: interlocked order.

nocturnōs . . . ignēs: a metaphor for the stars.

Aurōra, -ae, f., *the dawn, daybreak*; here personified, *Aurora* (goddess of the dawn).

82 *****sōl, sōlis**, m., *the sun*, or here (as in the tale of the Sun's loves that follows this story in the *Metamorphoses*) *Sol* (god of the sun).

pruīnōsus, -a, -um, *frosty.*

> **pruīnōsās . . . siccāverat herbās**: the word order replicates, and to an extent rhymes with, **nocturnōs . . . remōverat ignēs** (81), a typically Ovidian device.

*****radius, -ī**, m., *a ray of light.*

siccō, -āre, -āvī, -ātus, *to dry.*

83 **solitus, -a, -um**, *usual, accustomed.*

> Note the assonance of **-tum/-cum/Tum/murmure** and cf. line 70.

parvō: here, *gentle, quiet.*

84 **multa . . . silentī**: note the **s/t** alliteration and the internal rhyme, which is accentuated by the pauses after **questī** and **silentī**.

*****queror, querī, questus sum**, *to complain (about), protest.*

statuō, statuere, statuī, statūtus, *to set upright, stand*; with **ut** + subjn., *to decide (that).*

ut . . . temptent (85) **. . . relinquant** (86) **. . . conveniant . . . lateant** (88): jussive noun clauses (indirect commands) after **statuunt**.

silēns, silentis, *quiet, silent.*

85 **fallere custōdēs foribusque excēdere**: chiasmus, and a neat **f/c/d/f/c/d** alliteration; the infinitives are complementary to **temptent**.

foribus: sc. **ex** (prepositions expected in prose are frequently omitted in verse).

86 **tēctum, -ī**, n., *roof, ceiling; house, building* (a common synecdoche).

87 **nēve**, conj., *and so that . . . not* (introducing a negative purpose clause).

sit errandum: passive periphrastic, following **nēve** and with **spatiantibus** as dat. of agent, *so that they would not go astray* (lit., *so that it would not be gone astray by them*), *as they wander about in the vast countryside.*

lātus, -a, -um, *broad, wide; extensive, vast.*

spatior, -ārī, -ātus sum, *to walk* or *wander about.*

88 *****conveniō, convenīre, convēnī, conventūrus**, *to assemble, meet*; + dat., *to be suited (to), befit, harmonize (with).*

bustum, -ī, n., *funeral pyre; grave-mound, tomb* (here, poetic pl. for sing.).

Ninus, -ī, m., *Ninus* (king of Assyria, founder of Nineveh, and husband of Semiramis—see on 58 above).

89 **arboris**: the diaeresis, the word's enjambement, and its repetition as first word of the following parenthesis purposefully focus our attention on the tree which will be central to the story.

80   ōscula quisque suae nōn pervenientia contrā.
       "Postera nocturnōs Aurōra remōverat ignēs,
       Sōlque pruīnōsās radiīs siccāverat herbās;
       ad solitum coiēre locum. Tum, murmure parvō
       multa prius questī, statuunt ut nocte silentī
85   fallere custōdēs foribusque excēdere temptent,
       cumque domō exierint, urbis quoque tēcta relinquant,
       nēve sit errandum lātō spatiantibus arvō,
       conveniant ad busta Ninī, lateantque sub umbrā
       arboris (arbor ibī niveīs ūberrima pōmīs,
90   ardua mōrus, erat, gelidō contermina fontī).
       Pacta placent; et lūx, tardē discēdere vīsa,

Discussion Question

Comment on the onomatopoeia in 83. How may the alliteration in the
following verse also be onomatopoetic?

---

*niveus, -a, -um, (consisting) of snow; snow-white, snowy.
ūber, ūberis, copious, abundant; + abl., rich (in).
*pōmum, -ī, n., fruit-tree; fruit.
90 *arduus, -a, -um, tall, towering; steep, precipitous.
mōrus, -ī, f., mulberry tree.
*gelidus, -a, -um, cold, cool, chilly.
conterminus, -a, -um + dat., bordering (upon), close (to).
*fōns, fontis, m., a spring, spring-water.
91   pactum, -ī, n., agreement, plan.
      Pacta placent: sc. eīs, i.e., the lovers, although from the next verse and
      a half it appears that even nature is in accord with the plan; the short,
      alliterative sentence effectively punctuates the detailed plan preceding
      and introduces the scene shift following.
    et lūx . . . ab īsdem (92): a brilliantly economical description of sunset, with
      the sluggish spondees of 91 aptly giving way to the plummeting dactyls in
      92, the lūx/nox/exit soundplay, and the highly visual (and sonorous)
      chiasmus of praecipitātur aquīs et aquīs . . . exit.
    vīsa: having seemed (at first), i.e., to the lovers, who were eager for
      nightfall.

92 **praecipitō, -āre, -āvī, -ātus,** *to plunge* or *hurl downward* (in contrast to tardē discēdere).
     praecipitātur aquīs: sc. **in.**
  aquīs et aquīs: placement of **-quīs** under the ictus accentuates the rhyme.
  nox: the abrupt monosyllable (which echoes **lūx** in 91), and the diaeresis following, deliberately disturb the rhythm before bringing the scene to closure.
  īsdem: = **eīsdem;** *the same,* since in the mythic world ocean surrounded the lands in a continuous stream, out of which rose and set both daylight and darkness.

93 *callidus, -a, -um,** *expert, wise; clever, crafty* (here perhaps with adverbial force, *cunningly*).
  tenebrae, -ārum, f. pl., *darkness.*
  *verso, -āre, -āvī, -ātus,** *to turn, spin; to turn back and forth, twist.*
     versātō cardine: *turning the door on its hinges* (lit., *with the door-hinge turned*).
  cardō, cardinis, m., *pivot, axis; door-hinge.*

94 **suōs:** i.e., her family (cf. **fallere custōdēs** 85).
  adopertus, -a, -um, *covered, veiled.*
     adoperta: with **vultum,** acc. of respect, and modifying **Thisbē,** *with her face concealed* (with a shawl, see 101).

95 **pervenit . . . sēdit:** chiasmus.
  *tumulus, -ī,** m., *burial mound, tomb.*
  dictā . . . arbore: *the tree which they had spoken of.*

96 **audācem faciēbat amor:** sc. **eam;** this clause, one of Ovid's many epigrammatic **sententiae,** anticipates the boldness Thisbe will need for the action that follows.
  ecce, recentī / caede (97): the harsh alliteration helps compel our attention to the scene Ovid means us to visualize.
  *recēns, recentis,** *recent, newly arrived; newly shed; recently caught.*

97 *caedēs, caedis,** f., *killing, slaughter; blood, gore.*
  leaena, -ae, f., *lioness.*
  boum: gen. pl. of **bōs,** objective gen. with **caede.**
  spūmō, -āre, -āvī, -ātūrus, *to foam, be covered with foam.*
     spūmantēs . . . rictūs: acc. of respect with **oblita,** *her foaming jowls smeared.*
  oblinō, oblinere, oblēvī, oblitus, *to smear, cover.*
  rictus, -ūs, m., *the open mouth, jaws.*

98 **dēpositūra:** fut. act. participle, here with the force of purpose, *to slake, satisfy.*
  *sitis, sitis,** acc. **sitim,** f., *thirst.*

99 **Quam:** = **Eam,** the lioness.
  ad: here, *by the light of.*
  lūna, -ae, f., *the moon.*
  Babylōnius, -a, -um, *Babylonian.*

praecipitātur aquīs, et aquīs nox exit ab īsdem.
   "Callida per tenebrās, versātō cardine, Thisbē
ēgreditur, fallitque suōs, adopertaque vultum
95   pervenit ad tumulum, dictāque sub arbore sēdit—
audācem faciēbat amor. Venit, ecce, recentī
caede leaena boum spūmantēs oblita rictūs,
dēpositūra sitim vīcīnī fontis in undā.
   Quam procul ad lūnae radiōs Babylōnia Thisbē
100   vīdit et obscūrum timidō pede fūgit in antrum,

Discussion Questions

1.   How much time elapses between verses 81 and 92?

2.   Comment further on the several ways in which Ovid uses meter and word order to enhance the imagery in 91–92; what movements of light and darkness do we actually see and hear in these two lines?

3.   How does Ovid's description of the time and place of the lovers' rendezvous in 88–95 help to establish a mood of foreboding? How does the poet use images of light and dark in these lines; what, specifically, may be the symbolism of the lūx/nox antithesis in 91–92?

---

100   *obscūrus, -a, -um, *dark, obscure; shadowy; hidden from sight.*
        obscūrum . . . antrum: in a neat word-picture, the rest of the clause is actually "enclosed," like Thisbe herself, within *the shadowy cave;* again word order enhances imagery (cf. I.468 above). Note too the chiaroscuro effect, as Thisbe flees out of the shadows of the moonlit night into the cave's profounder darkness—an unpropitious omen of things to come.
     timidō pede fūgit: for the transferred epithet cf. timidō Pēnēia cursū / fūgit (I.525–26 above).
    antrum, -ī, n., *cave, cavern, grotto.*

101 **dumque fugit . . . relīquit**: the tense shift is usual with **dum**.

    tergō . . . lapsa: sc. **dē**; again English would use a clause (*which had slipped from her back*) rather than the more literal participial phrase (*having slipped from her back*).

    vēlāmina: here (as often) pl. for sing. (cf. **tenuēs . . . amictūs** 104).

102 **lea, -ae**, f., *lioness.*

    lea saeva . . . multā . . . undā: chiasmus.

    compēscō, compēscere, compēscuī, *to confine, restrain; to subdue, quench.*

103 **inventōs . . . amictūs** (104): notice how the noun and its modifier frame the lengthy clause (cf. **lētī . . . tuī** 151–52); for translation of the participle, see on **tergō . . . lapsa** (101).

    ipsā: i.e., Thisbe.

104 **cruentō, -āre, -āvī, -ātus**, *to stain with blood.*

    *__lāniō, -āre, -āvī, -ātus__, *to wound savagely; to tear, shred, mutilate.*

    *__amictus, -ūs__, m., *mantle, cloak.*

105 **ēgressus**: with **Pȳramus** (107).

106 **pulvis, pulveris**, m., *dust.*

    certa ferae: with **vestīgia**, delayed for suspense.

    tōtō . . . ōre: sc. **in**, but English would make *face* the subject (*his whole face grew pale*).

107 *__tingō, tingere, tīnxī, tīnctus__, *to wet, soak, moisten; to dye, stain, color.*

108 *__reperiō, reperīre, repperī, repertus__, *to find, discover; to find (someone, something) to be.*

109 **ē quibus**: partitive abl., *of whom.*

    illa: Thisbe.

    dignus, -a, -um, *suitable, appropriate*; + abl., *worthy (of).*

110 **nostra**: = **mea** (cf. **nostrum** 112, **nostrī** 118).

    nocēns: here, *guilty*, predicate adj.; and note the assonance with **nostra**.

    *__anima, -ae__, f., *air, breath; soul, life; spirit, ghost.*

    Ego tē: looking back to **illa** (109) and **nostra** (110), the pronouns are emphatically juxtaposed.

    miserandus, -a, -um, *pitiable.*

    perimō, perimere, perēmī, perēmptus, *to destroy, kill.*

111 **in loca plēna metūs**: with **venīrēs**; cf. **per . . . loca plēna timōris** (X.29 below).

    quī: **ego** (110) is the antecedent.

    venīrēs: sc. **ut**, a subjunctive jussive noun clause instead of the infinitive usual with **iubeō**.

112 **dīvellō, dīvellere, dīvellī, dīvulsus**, *to tear apart, tear to pieces.*

113 **scelerātus, -a, -um**, *accursed; criminal, sinful.*

    scelerāta . . . morsū: the interlocking order, with the powerful imperative at center, produces a symmetrical golden line—and the **scelerāta . . . viscera** are separated quite aptly, in view of the violence imagined in the equally powerful (and symmetrical) **Nostrum dīvellite corpus** (112).

dumque fugit, tergō vēlāmina lapsa relīquit.
Ut lea saeva sitim multā compēscuit undā,
dum redit in silvās, inventōs forte sine ipsā
ōre cruentātō tenuēs laniāvit amictūs.

105   "Sērius ēgressus, vestīgia vīdit in altō
pulvere certa ferae, tōtōque expalluit ōre
Pȳramus; ut vērō vestem quoque sanguine tīnctam
repperit, 'Ūna duōs,' inquit, 'nox perdet amantēs,
ē quibus illa fuit longā dignissima vītā;
110 nostra nocēns anima est. Ego tē, miseranda, perēmī,
in loca plēna metūs quī iussī nocte venīrēs
nec prior hūc vēnī. Nostrum dīvellite corpus,
et scelerāta ferō cōnsūmite viscera morsū,
ō quīcumque sub hāc habitātis rūpe leōnēs!

Discussion Questions

1.   How does Ovid make the scene in 96–101 more vivid and even visual? Consider especially his choice and manipulation of the verbs in the passage.

2.   What is especially effective about the poet's handling of Pyramus' name in the scene change at 105–07?

3.   What is the effect of the word order in 108 (**Ūna . . . amantēs**), and how does **nox perdet amantēs** continue the light/dark symbolism of 88–93? If you have read Catullus 5, what connections of theme and imagery do you see between that poem and these verses, especially 108?

---

*ferus, -a, -um, *wild; ferocious, savage.*
cōnsūmō, cōnsūmere, cōnsūmpsī, cōnsūmptus, *to destroy; to devour.*
viscus, visceris, n., usually pl., *flesh, entrails.*
114   ō, interj. used in direct address or exclamations, *oh* (here introducing a dramatic apostrophe).
*quīcumque, quaecumque, quodcumque, indefinite adj. or pron., *whoever, whatever* (here with **leōnēs**).
rūpēs, rūpis, f., *a rocky cliff, crag.*

115 **timidī est**: gen. of characteristic, *it is (the mark) of a cowardly (man)*.
 *****nex, necis**, f., *death, murder*.
116 **pactus, -a, -um**, *agreed upon, settled upon* (with **arboris**).
 umbram: again the poet focuses on the dark shadow cast beneath the tree, to intensify the atmosphere of foreboding (cf. 88–89 above).
117 **nōtae . . . vestī**: indirect object with the repeated verb and both direct objects; for the anaphora (here with a pathetic effect) and the word order, cf. I.458 above.
118 **haustus, -ūs**, m., *drink, draft*.
119 **Quōque**: = rel. pron. **quō** (with **ferrum** as antecedent) + **que**.
 accingō, accingere, accīnxī, accīnctus, *to gird, equip*.
 dēmīsit: here, *plunged*.
 īlia, īlium, n. pl., *groin, genitals; entrails*.
 *****ferrum, -ī**, n., *iron*; by synecdoche, *weapon, sword* (with both **dēmīsit** and **trāxit** 120).
120 *****mora, -ae**, f., *delay*; **nec mora**, idiom, *and without delay* (cf. *Am.* I.11.19 below—and note the assonance here with **moriēns**).
 fervēns, ferventis, *boiling; warm* (here, with freshly shed blood).
121 **resupīnus, -a, -um**, *lying flat on one's back*.
 humus, -ī, f., *the earth, ground* (with the abl. here sc. **in**—prose would normally have the locative **humī** instead).
 *****cruor, cruōris**, m., *blood* (from a wound); *slaughter*.
 ēmicō, -āre, -āvī, -ātūrus, *to move suddenly outward* or *upward; to spurt out* or *upward*.
122 *****aliter**, adv., *otherwise, differently*; **nōn aliter quam cum**, *no differently than when* (= *just as when*), a conventional formula for introducing a simile (cf. *Met.* X.64–65 below).
 vitiātus, -a, -um, *faulty, defective* (like the wall that separated the lovers' houses—cf. *vitium* 67).
 fistula, -ae, f., *tube, pipe* (especially, as here, *a water-pipe*).
123 **scinditur . . . / ēiaculātur . . . rumpit** (124): the strong verbs are emphatically positioned, the last two in a chiastic arrangement with their objects.
 strīdō, strīdere, strīdī, *to hiss*.
 forāmen, forāminis, n., *a hole, perforation*.
 longās / . . . aquās (124): *long streams of water*.
124 **ēiaculor, ēiaculārī, ēiaculātus sum**, *to shoot out, discharge*.
 ictus, -ūs, m., *a stroke, blow*; here, *spurt, pulsing*.
125 **arboreus, -a, -um**, *of a tree*.
 *****fētus, -ūs**, m., *giving birth; fruit; offspring* (*fruit* here, but in view of the overt sexual imagery of the preceding lines, there is clearly a double entendre suggesting the children the two lovers will never have).
 adspergō, adsperginis, f., *sprinkling, spattering*.
 *****āter, ātra, ātrum**, *black, dark*.
126 *****vertō, vertere, vertī, versus**, *to* (cause to) *turn, spin; to reverse, change*.
 *****faciēs, -ēī**, f., *outward appearance; face; shape, form*.
 madefactus, -a, -um, *drenched, soaked*.

115   Sed timidī est optāre necem.' Vēlāmina Thisbēs
       tollit, et ad pactae sēcum fert arboris umbram,
       utque dedit nōtae lacrimās, dedit ōscula vestī,
       'Accipe nunc,' inquit, 'nostrī quoque sanguinis haustūs!'
       Quōque erat accīnctus, dēmīsit in īlia ferrum,
120   nec mora, ferventī moriēns ē vulnere trāxit,
       et iacuit resupīnus humō. Cruor ēmicat altē,
       nōn aliter quam cum vitiātō fistula plumbō
       scinditur, et tenuī strīdente forāmine longās
       ēiaculātur aquās, atque ictibus āera rumpit.
125   Arboreī fētūs adspergine caedis in ātram
       vertuntur faciem, madefactaque sanguine rādīx

Discussion Questions

1.   What is Pyramus addressing in 118? What is the point of **quoque**? What is the emotional effect of this and the preceding line?

2.   Comment on the effect of the **c/q** alliteration in 118–19.

3.   What is striking in the meter of 121 and how is it appropriate to the action described?

4.   One commentary (DeVeau and Getty) calls the comparison in 122–24 "certainly one of Ovid's least attractive similes." Is the simile effective or not?

5.   Comment on the alliteration and assonance in 123; is an onomatopoetic effect intended? And what of the sound effects in 124?

Pyramus: Now am I dead,
                    Now am I fled;
             My soul is in the sky:
                    Tongue, lose thy light;
                    Moon, take thy flight:
             Now, die, die, die, die, die.

William Shakespeare
A Midsummer Night's Dream
Act V, Sc. I

127 **purpureus, -a, -um**, *purple*.

  purpureō . . . colōre: the adjective/noun pair frame the line, emphasizing the dark transformation of the fruit and vividly bringing the scene to closure; the assonance of ō/ō/ō (under the ictus in each instance) adds a suitably doleful tone.

  mōrum, -ī, n., *a mulberry*.

  *****color, colōris**, m., *color*.

128 **positō**: = **dēpositō**.

  nē fallat: the purpose clause is dependent on **redit** (129).

129 **animō**: here, *heart*.

  requīrō, requīrere, requīsīvī, requīsītus, *to try to find, search for; to need, miss, long for* (here, through zeugma, the first sense is required with **oculīs** and the second with **animō**).

130 **vītārit**: = **vītāverit**, perf. subjn. in the indirect question (for the syncopated form, cf. **agitāsse** I.567 above) .

  gestiō, gestīre, gestīvī, *to desire eagerly, long*.

131 **Utque . . . / sīc** (132): here, as often, with an implied contrast, *and although . . . at the same time*.

  vīsā: with **arbore**; English would use a clause, *once she has seen it*.

  in arbore fōrmam: = **fōrmam arboris**.

132 **facit**: sc. **eam**.

  *****incertus, -a, -um**, *not fixed; uncertain, doubtful; disarranged*.

  color: suspensefully held to the end of the clause and followed by a strong diaeresis.

  haeret: here, *she is uncertain* (cf. the similar English idiom, *to be stuck*, i.e., *puzzled*, over some problem).

  haeret an haec sit: sc. **arbor**; the harsh sounds (like the **c**'s in the first part of the line) and the uneven rhythm caused by the closing series of monosyllables help suggest Thisbe's hesitance to approach the tree.

133 *****dubitō, -āre, -āvī, -ātus**, *to be in doubt* or *uncertain* (with **an** + indirect question); *to waver, hesitate*.

  tremebundus, -a, -um, *quivering, trembling*.

  tremebunda . . . cruentum / membra solum (134): interlocked order, with the epithets first, to focus on the grisly aspects of the scene. While **tremebunda** could refer to Thisbe as subject of **dubitat** and **videt** (cf. **tremit** 136), the connection with **pulsāre** makes its application to **membra** more likely—or, through a common poetic device, Ovid might well intend us to take the word in both ways.

  *****pulsō, -āre, -āvī, -ātus**, *to strike, beat (against)*.

  cruentus, -a, -um, *bloody*.

134 **membra**: at first Thisbe notices merely the body itself, only later (137) recognizing it as that of her lover.

  solum, -ī, n., *base, foundation; ground, earth*.

  retrōque pedem tulit: i.e., *she stepped back*.

  ōraque . . . gerēns (135): *and with her face* (lit., *wearing a facial expression*).

purpureō tingit pendentia mōra colōre.
    "Ecce, metū nōndum positō, nē fallat amantem,
illa redit, iuvenemque oculīs animōque requīrit,
130   quantaque vītārit narrāre perīcula gestit.
Utque locum et vīsā cognōscit in arbore fōrmam,
sīc facit incertam pōmī color; haeret an haec sit.
Dum dubitat, tremebunda videt pulsāre cruentum
membra solum, retrōque pedem tulit, ōraque buxō
135   pallidiōra gerēns exhorruit aequoris īnstar,
quod tremit, exiguā cum summum stringitur aurā.

Discussion Questions

1.   Ancient epic often contained seemingly gratuitous descriptions of physical violence; how is Ovid's graphic depiction of Pyramus' suicide (in 118–27), on the other hand, quite essential to the story-line?

2.   The tree's berries turn dark from two different causes in 125–27; comment on the two images and their "believability."

3.   How does Ovid introduce an element of bittersweet irony in the scene-change at 128–30?

4.   In what way is the meter in the first half of 133 appropriate to the actions described? Comment on the line's other sound effects.

5.   How is Ovid's description of Thisbe's face in 134–35 especially apt in this context?

6.   Comment on the simile in 135–36.

---

       buxus, -ī, f., *the box-tree; boxwood* (noted for its pale color).
135   **pallidus, -a, -um**, *pale, colorless.*
       exhorrēscō, exhorrēscere, exhorruī, *to shudder, shiver* (with fear).
       aequor, aequoris, n., *a smooth, level surface; the surface of the sea* (especially when calm).
       īnstar, indecl. n. noun, *the equivalent (of)*; here, with **aequoris**, *just like the sea.*
136   **exiguus, -a, -um**, *small, slight.*
       cum: in prose this conjunction (*when*) would introduce the clause.
       summum: here substantive, *its surface.*

137   **remoror, remorārī, remorātus sum,** *to delay, pause.*

138   **clārus, -a, -um,** *loud, sonorous; clear.*

        plangor, plangōris, m., *beating of the breast* (as a sign of grief); *lamentation, wailing.*

139   **comās:** acc. of respect with **laniāta.**

140   **vulnera . . . lacrimīs, flētum . . . cruōrī:** chiasmus.

        suppleō, supplēre, supplēvī, supplētus, *to fill up* (with a liquid).

        flētus, -ūs, m., *weeping, lamentation; tears.*

        cruōrī: prose would have the abl. case.

142   **Pȳrame . . . tē . . . / Pȳrame . . . tē** (143): the repetitions, identically placed in the two verses, intensify the pathos, and the names in particular help create an incantatory effect as well.

        quis: with **cāsus,** instead of the interrogative adj. **quī.**

        mihi: dat. of reference, with the sense of separation.

        *cāsus, -ūs, m., *a fall; mishap, misfortune, accident.*

        adimō, adimere, adēmī, adēmptus, *to remove, take away.*

143   **respondē . . . iacentēs** (144): the -dē/tē/-bē assonance, the strong **d/t** alliteration in both verses, and the series of spondees following **nōminat,** all lend a forceful sound effect to Thisbe's imperatives.

144   **exaudiō, -īre, -īvī, -ītus,** *to hear; to listen to, heed.*

        *attollō, attollere, *to raise, lift up.*

        iacentēs: lit., *lying (still);* here, *motionless, lifeless.*

145   **Ad nōmen Thisbēs:** Thisbe had repeatedly called her lover's name to arouse him (note the careful positioning of **Pȳrame . . . / Pȳrame . . . / nōminat** 142–44), but it was the sound of her own name (also deliberately set at line's end in 143) that momentarily revived him.

        nōmen . . . oculōs . . . gravātōs: again the ō/ō/ō assonance adds a mournful sound effect (cf. on 127).

        oculōs . . . gravātōs: object of both **ērēxit** and **recondidit** (146).

        morte: in order to appreciate fully what is happening in this scene, it is important to note that Pyramus is now dead (cf. **gelidīs in vultibus** 141) or at least hovering very near the brink of death.

        gravō, -āre, -āvī, -ātus, *to make heavy, weigh down; to oppress, overwhelm.*

146   **Pȳramus:** again the name is emphatically positioned (cf. 142–43).

        ērigō, ērigere, ērēxī, ērēctus, *to raise, lift up.*

        vīsā . . . illā: abl. absolute.

        recondō, recondere, recondidī, reconditus, *to put away, store; to put back, close again.*

147   **Quae:** = **Illa** (cf. **illā** preceding), subject of **inquit** (148).

        postquam vestemque suam: placement of **-am/-em/-am** under the ictus accentuates the assonance.

        postquam . . . suam cognōvit: an echo of 137, where the words appear in the same metrical position.

        vestem . . . cognōvit . . . / vīdit ebur (148): chiasmus.

        -que . . . et: = **-que . . . -que,** *both . . . and.*

        ēnsis, ēnsis, m., *sword.*

Sed postquam, remorāta, suōs cognōvit amōrēs,
percutit indignōs clārō plangōre lacertōs
et, laniāta comās amplexaque corpus amātum,
140 vulnera supplēvit lacrimīs, flētumque cruōrī
miscuit, et gelidīs in vultibus ōscula fīgēns
'Pȳrame,' clāmāvit, 'quis tē mihi cāsus adēmit?
Pȳrame, respondē! Tua tē, cārissime, Thisbē
nōminat; exaudī vultūsque attolle iacentēs!'
145 Ad nōmen Thisbēs oculōs iam morte gravātōs
Pȳramus ērēxit, vīsāque recondidit illā.
    "Quae, postquam vestemque suam cognōvit et ēnse
vīdit ebur vacuum, 'Tua tē manus,' inquit, 'amorque

Discussion Questions

1. What sound is most strikingly repeated in 137–38 and how is the effect
   onomatopoetic? How does Ovid's manipulation of ictus enhance this effect?

2. How is the chiastic arrangement in 140 suited to the image being described?

3. In Roman magic (officially discouraged, but in fact practiced from the
   earliest times and throughout the imperial period), personal names were felt
   to have a special power and so they were often repeated in curses and other
   incantations; control of the name suggested potential control of the person.
   With this in mind, consider carefully the scene in 142–46 and discuss how it
   may be construed, at least on one level, as a kind of magical rite.

ēnse / . . . vacuum (148): abl. of separation, *empty of its sword*.

148 **vīdit . . . amorque**: the quick dactyls are appropriate to Thisbe's agitated
state.

*ebur, eboris, n., *ivory*; by synecdoche, *an object made of ivory* (here, *an
ivory scabbard*).

Tua tē: an echo of the identically positioned **Tua tē** in 143.

manus . . . amorque: the two instruments of Pyramus' death are one
concrete and the other abstract.

149   **perdidit**: sing. to agree with only the nearer of the two subjects.

    *īnfēlīx, īnfēlīcis, *unfertile, unproductive; disastrous, ill-fated, unfortunate* (most editors set the adjective off with a comma here, regarding it as vocative, but **amor . . . īnfēlīx** is more effective and likelier what Ovid intended).

    Est . . . manus (150): freely, *My hand too has the courage for this one act.*

    et: = **etiam** (likewise in the next verse).

    in ūnum / hoc (150): i.e., for suicide.

150   **est et amor**: the phrase, like **Est et . . . manus**, is to be taken with **mihi fortis in ūnum / hoc**, a dat. of possession construction; the anaphora focuses our attention back on **manus . . . amorque** (148).

    dabit . . . vīrēs: thus Thisbe's love (**hic**) is likewise **īnfēlīx**, i.e., it will beget death and not new life—except, of course, in the **fētūs** (161) of the mulberry tree.

    hic: though the vowel is short, the syllable was often treated in verse as long (owing to an earlier form **hicc**); cf. **hoc** in *Am.* I.1.5 below.

    in vulnera: i.e., like **in ūnum / hoc**, *for death.*

151   **persequor, persequī, persecūtus sum**, *to follow to the end; to pursue.*

    exstīnctum: here, *dead* or *in death*; sc. **tē** (i.e., Pyramus).

    *lētum, -ī, n., *death, destruction.*

        lētī . . . tuī (152): noun and adj. frame the clause (cf. **inventōs . . . amictūs** 103–04).

152   **quīque**: sc. **tū** as antecedent.

    revellō, revellere, revellī, revulsus, *to tear away, remove forcibly.*

153   **sōlā**: with **morte** not **mē** (152).

    nec: here, *not even.*

154   **Hoc . . . estōte rogātī, / . . . / ut** (156): the pronoun is object of this rare future imperative construction, which has a solemn, almost ritualistic tone, *You shall be asked this one request . . . that.*

    ambōrum: i.e., of both Pyramus and Thisbe.

155   **multum**: adv. with **miserī**.

    meus: masculine sing. because she thinks only of her father's prohibition (cf. **vetuēre patrēs** 61); alliteration of **m** in the first half of the line adds a somber tone to the pitiful apostrophe.

156   **ut . . . eōdem** (157): the entire clause is in apposition to **hoc** (see on 154), elaborating Thisbe's entreaty; note the heavy assonance of **ō** in these two verses.

    quōs: sc. **nōs** (the two lovers) as both antecedent of this relative pronoun (which is repeated for pathetic effect) and subject of the infin. **compōnī** (157); the request is essentially **ut nōs, quōs amor iūnxit, in eōdem tumulō compōnī nōn invideātis**.

    certus amor . . . hōra novissima: chiasmus underscores the ironic contrast between the steadfastness of the lovers' affection and their sudden reversal of fortune.

    novissima: here, *most recent, last.*

157   **compōnī**: here, with **nōs** understood, *us to be placed together*, i.e., *buried.*

perdidit īnfēlīx! Est et mihi fortis in ūnum
150   hoc manus, est et amor; dabit hic in vulnera vīrēs.
Persequar exstīnctum, lētīque miserrima dīcar
causa comesque tuī; quīque ā mē morte revellī
heu sōlā poterās, poteris nec morte revellī.
Hoc tamen ambōrum verbīs estōte rogātī,
155   ō multum miserī meus illīusque parentēs,
ut quōs certus amor, quōs hōra novissima iūnxit,
compōnī tumulō nōn invideātis eōdem.
At tū, quae rāmīs arbor miserābile corpus
nunc tegis ūnīus, mox es tēctūra duōrum,

Discussion Questions

1.   What is the intended effect of the anaphora **Est et . . . manus, est et amor** (149–50)?

2.   What is most striking in the language of 152–53 and what is the poet's purpose?

3.   What is unusual in the meter of 158 and how is the rhythm suited to the action at this point in the narrative?

---

invideō, invidēre, invīdī, invīsus, *to envy; to be unwilling to allow, refuse, begrudge.*
    nōn invideātis: with **ut**, a jussive noun clause (where **nē** would be the usual negative), *that you not be unwilling to allow.*
158   **At tū, quae rāmīs arbor:** having addressed first Pyramus, then (by apostrophe) their parents, Thisbe now suddenly turns to the tree itself, which had become their rendezvous for death, and speaks to it as though it were a sentient being; the direct address and the feminine modifiers (**quae** 158, **tēctūra** 159) create an impression of the tree as a woman. In prose (and in English translation) **arbor** would ordinarily precede **quae**, but here the antecedent is attracted into the relative clause.
    miserābile corpus: object both of **tegis** and (with the pl. **corpora** understood) of **es tēctūra** (159).
159   **es tēctūra:** fut. act. periphrastic, essentially = **tegēs.**

160   **signa tenē . . . habē fētūs** (161): chiasmus.

    pullus, -a, -um: *dark, dreary-colored* (used especially of the clothing worn by mourners).

    lūctus, -ūs, m., *(the expression of) grief, mourning, lamentation*.

    *****aptus, -a, -um**, *tied, bound*; + dat., *suitable (for)*.

161   **fētūs**: the object is held suspensefully to the end and has an array of connotations; the tree's fruits are "her" offspring (see on **fētūs** 125 and **īnfēlīx** 149) and, with **pullōs . . . et lūctibus aptōs** (160), they are also her dark cloak of mourning.

    *****geminus, -a, -um**, *twin-born, twin; twofold, double*.

    monimentum, -ī, n., *monument; token, reminder*.

162   **aptātō . . . īmum**: interlocked order.

    mūcrō, mūcrōnis, m., *the sharp end of a sword, point*.

    *****īmus, -a, -um**, *lowest, bottommost; the bottom of, base of*; n. pl. substantive, *the Underworld*.

163   *****incumbō, incumbere, incubuī** + dat., *to bend over; to throw oneself (on), fall (on), lie down (on)*.

        incubuit . . . tepēbat: strong verbs frame the line, and the harsh **c/d/t** alliteration suggests the violence of the act.

    *****tepeō, -ēre**, *to be warm; to have the warmth of a human body*.

164   **deōs . . . parentēs**: in an elaborate chiasmus, line 165 presents the gods' response, and line 166 the parents', to Thisbe's two entreaties, the first in 156–57 directed to the lovers' parents, and the second in 158–61 directed to the tree itself but answerable only through divine agency.

165   **permātūrēscō, permātūrēscere, permātūruī**, *to become fully ripe*.

        permātūruit, āter: the **-ātūr-/āter** soundplay is deliberate and typically Ovidian.

166   **quod**: sc. **id** (i.e., the lovers' cremated remains) as both antecedent of **quod** and subject of **requiēscit**.

    rogus, -ī, m., *funeral pyre* (here sc. **ex**).

        rogīs . . . urnā: alliteration of **r** and the assonance of **ūnā/urnā** lend a composed sound effect to the tale's closing verse.

    supersum, superesse, superfuī, irreg., *to be above; to remain, be left over*.

        superest: the word's final syllable, coming before the principal caesura and under the ictus, produces a deliberate internal rhyme with the identically positioned **est** in the preceding verse.

    *****requiēscō, requiēscere, requiēvī, requiētūrus**, *to rest, lie at rest*.

    *****urna, -ae**, f., *a pitcher, urn* (here, *a cinerary urn*).

Two, by themselves, each other, love and feare
Slaine, cruell friends, by parting have joyn'd here.

John Donne

160   signa tenē caedis pullōsque et lūctibus aptōs
      semper habē fētūs, geminī monimenta cruōris.'
        "Dīxit et, aptātō pectus mūcrōne sub īmum,
      incubuit ferrō, quod adhūc ā caede tepēbat.
      Vōta tamen tetigēre deōs, tetigēre parentēs:
165   nam color in pōmō est, ubi permātūruit, āter,
      quodque rogīs superest, ūnā requiēscit in urnā."

Discussion Questions

1.   Comment on the structure, metrics, and other special effects in 164.

2.   In what ways do the story's closing lines (165–66) aptly conclude the darkness/death imagery which Ovid has developed throughout the narrative?

3.   What similarities do you see between the ending of this tale and that of Daphne and Apollo? And what are some of the most significant differences?

4.   In what respects is this story more believable than the Daphne tale? How does it reveal Ovid's interest in "private versus public"?

"Pyramus and Thisbe"
Lucas Cranach the Elder, 1520-25
Staatsgalerie, Bamberg, Germany

ORPHEUS AND EURYDICE

Metamorphoses X.1–77

The tragic story of the singer Orpheus (son of the Muse Calliope) and his beloved wife Eurydice, twice lost to death, is certainly one of the best known of ancient myths. Ovid's version is told, with remarkable (and intentionally ill-proportioned) economy, in fewer than 80 lines: On the couple's wedding day, the hero's new bride falls dead, stricken by the bite of a serpent. Having mourned Eurydice "sufficiently" and "so that he might not neglect to try the shades of Hell"—two of several deliberately curious details in the narrative—Orpheus descends into the Underworld and appeals to Persephone and the prince of darkness to allow his wife's return to the land of the living. With a rambling, highly rhetorical lyric that takes up nearly a third of the entire tale, the minstrel, who could charm animals and even stones with his song, literally stupefies all the bloodless souls of Hades (the Danaids leave off carrying their urns and Sisyphus sits down on his rock!) and instantly compels Hades' king and queen to his will, on the condition, however, that in leading Eurydice out of their realm he should never look back at her face. Just as they reach the edge of upper earth, of course, Orpheus does steal a fateful backward glance, only to see Eurydice at that moment, "dying again," tumbling downward and for eternity into the abyss. Briefly stupefied himself at the calamity, and then thwarted in his attempt at a second crossing of the river Styx, Orpheus retreats to the mountains of his homeland Thrace (despite the implications of an earlier pledge to join his wife in death should he fail in his mission).

The story was in antiquity widely known from several versions, in particular from Vergil's *Georgics* (IV.452–546), and modern readers ought to consider carefully the differences between the two accounts, just as Ovid expected his contemporary audience to do. Suffice it here to say that Vergil's protagonist is at once more heroic and more sympathetic, his Eurydice far more dimensional (in Ovid's telling, the hapless bride is a mere sketch of a character and has but a single word to say, *Valē*), his rendering of Hell more fearful (and never verging on the comic, like Sisyphus perched on his stone). In Vergil's concluding scene, Orpheus' head, torn from his shoulders by a throng of crazed Bacchantes and hurled into the Hebrus river, cried out the name of his beloved Eurydice again and again as it floated downstream, a pitiable lament re-echoed by the river's banks. In Ovid's anti-epic version, a clever undercutting of the traditional tale, Eurydice, "sufficiently mourned," seems insufficiently loved, and his magniloquent Orpheus seems closer in his ineptitudes to Daphne's blustering Apollo than to Thisbe's Pyramus, whose actions speak, as properly they should, far louder than his words.

Like the other transformations in this book, Eurydice's ill-fated marriage to the mystical lord of song and her tragic metamorphosis from dead to dead again have fascinated musicians, poets, and artists over the centuries. The story has inspired verse by Wordsworth and Shelley (both of whom looked to Vergil's account), Swinburne and Robert Browning, Rilke, D.H. Lawrence, Robert Lowell, and James Dickey; operas by Jacopo Peri (our earliest surviving opera, first performed in 1600) and Claudio Monteverdi (1607), by Gluck and Haydn and Mozart in the 18th century, by Offenbach in the 19th, and even the modern Japanese opera, *Hiroshima no Orfe* (*Orpheus in Hiroshima*), by Yasushi Akutagawa (1967); other musical compositions by Schubert and Liszt and Stravinsky; numerous dramatizations, including Henry Fielding's farce, *Eurydice, or, The Devil Henpeck'd* (1737), Jean Anouilh's *Eurydice* (1941), and Tennessee Williams' *Orpheus Descending* (1955); paintings by Titian, Poussin, Rubens, and Feuerbach (seen below); sculpture by Bandinelli and Rodin; and a wide range of other artistic productions, among them three choreographed dances by Isadora Duncan and the films *Orphée* (1949) and *Le Testament d'Orphée* (1959) by Jean Cocteau and Marcel Camus' *Black Orpheus* (1959).

"Orpheus and Eurydice"
Anselm Feuerbach, 1869
Österreichische Galerie
Vienna

1 **Inde**: Book IX had ended with the wedding of Iphis and Ianthe on the island
of Crete; the marriage god Hymenaeus (line 2) now makes his way from
that event to the wedding of Orpheus and Eurydice.
immēnsus, -a, -um, *boundless, vast* (with **aethera** 2).
croceus, -a, -um, *of saffron; saffron-colored, yellow* (the color worn by
brides in Roman weddings).
   croceō . . . amictū: the words surround **vēlātus** just as the cloak itself
      was wrapped around the god.
vēlō, -āre, -āvī, -ātus, *to cover, clothe* (with **Hymenaeus** 2).
2 **aethēr, aetheris**, acc. **aethera**, n., *the upper regions of space, heaven.*
dīgredior, dīgredī, dīgressūrus, *to go away, depart.*
Cicōnēs, Cicōnum, m. pl., *the Cicones* (a tribe of southern Thrace).
Hymenaeus, -ī, m., *the Greek wedding refrain; the god of marriage* (cf.
   Hymēn I.480).
*****ōra, -ae**, f., *shore, coast.*
3 *****tendō, tendere, tetendī, tentus**, *to extend, stretch forth; to proceed.*
Orphēus, -a, -um, *of* or *belonging to Orpheus.*
   Orphēā . . . vōce: Ovid uses the adjective instead of Orpheus' name, in
      order to focus on the man's most remarkable attribute, his
      mesmerizing voice (which in this case fails to achieve the effect he
      desired); cf. **Rhodopēius . . . vātēs** (11–12).
nēquīquam: because, while Hymenaeus did appear, his epiphany proved
   most unpropitious.
4 **ille**: Hymenaeus.
nec . . . / nec . . . nec (5): an effective polysyndeton.
sollemnis, -is, -e, *ceremonial, ritual; traditional.*
   sollemnia verba: i.e., the wedding hymn.
5 **nec . . . fēlīx**: a heavy spondaic line, with conflict of ictus and accent.
*****ōmen, ōminis**, n., *omen, augury, sign.*
6 **quoque quam**: note the alliteration and cf. **ūsque/-ōsque** in the next line.
lacrimōsus, -a, -um, *tearful; causing tears.*
   lacrimōsō . . . fūmō: the repeated ō's are perhaps meant as a mournful
      sound effect.
strīdulus, -a, -um, *shrill, high-pitched* (here, *hissing* or *sputtering*, a sound
   further suggested by the repeated s's in 6–7).
7 *****ūsque**, adv., *all the way to* or *from; continuously.*
   nūllōs . . . ignēs: i.e., the torch was sputtering and smoking (irritating the
      eyes of the celebrants) and never thoroughly caught fire, even as it was
      waved back and forth to ignite the sparks.
mōtus, -ūs, m., *movement* (here, *even with shaking*).
8 **exitus, -ūs**, m., *departure, exit; outcome.*
   Exitus . . . gravior: sc. **fuit**; brevity, ellipsis, and the quick dactyls add
      point to the **sententia**.
*****auspicium, -ī**, n., *omen, augury* (here abl. of comparison).
Nam . . . vagātur (9): there are some striking sound effects, including

Inde per immēnsum, croceō vēlātus amictū,
aethera dīgreditur Ciconumque Hymenaeus ad ōrās
tendit, et Orphēā nēquīquam vōce vocātur.
Adfuit ille quidem, sed nec sollemnia verba
5   nec laetōs vultūs nec fēlīx attulit ōmen;
fax quoque, quam tenuit, lacrimōsō strīdula fūmō
ūsque fuit nūllōsque invēnit mōtibus ignēs.
Exitus auspiciō gravior. Nam nūpta per herbās
dum nova, Nāiadum turbā comitāta, vagātur,

Discussion Questions

1. How is the positioning of **immēnsum** . . . / **aethera** (1–2) appropriate to the scene described?

2. How does meter reinforce meaning in verses 2–3? What is especially effective in the shift of rhythm in 3?

3. Comment on the wordplay in **vōce vocātur** (3).

4. What are the multiple effects of the meter, the polysyndeton, and the positioning of the adjectives in 4–5?

5. How does the ominous scene conjured up by **lacrimōsō . . . fūmō** (6) foreshadow the events that follow?

6. Notice that Eurydice is at first (like Orpheus) not named, but only referred to as **nūpta . . . nova** (8–9); knowing that Ovid's audience was already well familiar with the story, what do you see as the effect?

alliteration of **n** and **t**, the assonance of **per/her-**, **dum/-dum**, and the series of **ā**'s, especially in **comitāta vagātur**.

nūpta, -ae, f., *a married woman, wife*; with **nova**, *a bride*.

9   **dum:** as often, the conjunction (which we should expect to precede **nūpta**) is delayed; cf. the position of **postquam** (11).

Nāias, Nāiadis, f., *a Naiad (a river nymph)*.

vagor, vagārī, vagātus sum, *to wander, roam*.

10   occidō, occidere, occidī, occāsūrus, *to fall, collapse; to die.*
        tālus, -ī, m., *ankle-bone, ankle.*
           in tālum . . . receptō: lit., *with a snake's tooth received into her ankle*;
           even in Latin the circumlocution is rather odd, as are other aspects of
           the narrative.
        dēns, dentis, m., *tooth, fang* (note the assonance in **serpentis dente**).

11   **Quam**: = **Eam**, object of **dēflēvit** (12); Eurydice, like Orpheus, is still not
        named (their names are delayed to verses 31 and 64, respectively). Note
        the internal rhyme **Quam . . . -rās** (at the caesura) **-quam . . . -rās**.
        satis: a curious modifier (did Orpheus mourn Eurydice just "enough"?), one
        of several elements in the narrative which Ovid deliberately introduces to
        undercut, and even burlesque, Orpheus' heroic image.
        *****superus, -a, -um, *above, upper.*
           ad superās . . . aurās: freely, *in the air above*, i.e., *in the upper world*;
           the alliteration of **s** in this verse (seven times) may onomatopoetically
           suggest the swirling of the winds on earth, in opposition to the stillness
           of the Underworld. Cf. **superā . . . ōrā** (26).
        *****Rhodopēius, -a, -um, *of Mt. Rhodope* (in Thrace, Orpheus' homeland).
           Rhodopēius . . . vātēs (12): for the epic circumlocution cf. 50 below.

12   dēfleō, dēflēre, dēflēvī, dēflētus, *to weep for, mourn.*
        *****vātēs, vātis, m., *prophet; bard, poet* (the word suggests divine inspiration,
        aptly of Orpheus, whose songs had mystical effect; cf. *Am.* III.15.1
        below).
        nē nōn temptāret: *that he might not fail to try*; a slightly odd double
        negative formulation (see on verse 25).
        et: = **etiam**, with **umbrās**, the antithesis of **aurās** (11).

13   Styx, Stygis, acc. **Styga**, f., *the Styx* (principal river of the Underworld) or,
        by metonymy, *the Underworld.*
        Taenarius, -a, -um, *of Taenarus* (a promontory in the southern Peloponnese,
        legendary site of a cave leading into Hades).
           Taenariā . . . portā: abl. of route (common with words like **porta,**
           terra, and **via**).

14   levēs populōs: here, *thin* or even *weightless tribes*, i.e., ghosts.
        *****simulācrum, -ī, n., *likeness; image, statue; phantom, ghost.*
           simulācra . . . fūncta sepulcrō: *phantoms of the dead* (lit., *ghosts that*
           have suffered burial).
        *****fungor, fungī, fūnctus sum + abl., *to perform; to experience, suffer* (with
        morte and similar words, *to die*).

15   Persephonē, Persephonēs, acc. **Persephonēn**, f., *Persephone* or *Proserpina*
        (daughter of Zeus and Demeter, wife of Pluto, and queen of the
        Underworld).
           Persephonēn . . . dominum (16): sc. **ad** with each noun.
        adiīt: the final **i**, normally short, is here lengthened under the ictus and
        before the caesura (diastole).
        inamoenus, -a, -um, *unpleasant, unlovely.*

10   occidit in tālum serpentis dente receptō.
      Quam satis ad superās postquam Rhodopēius aurās
    dēflēvit vātēs, nē nōn temptāret et umbrās,
    ad Styga Taenariā est ausus dēscendere portā,
    perque levēs populōs simulācraque fūncta sepulcrō
15   Persephonēn adiīt inamoenaque rēgna tenentem
    umbrārum dominum, pulsīsque ad carmina nervīs

Discussion Questions

1.   What effect does Ovid achieve through the enjambement of **occidit** (10) and the shift of meter following? Comment too on the line's striking **c/d/t** alliteration; are these sounds appropriate to the context?

2.   What is your response to Ovid's quick narration of Eurydice's death and Orpheus' mourning before descending into the underworld (10–12)? Is the narrative too abbreviated and the transition in 11 deliberately abrupt, and, if so, what is the poet's intent?

3.   How might the negative phrasing of the purpose clause in 12 serve to undercut Orpheus' heroic image?

4.   How is the meter in 12 suited to the scene shift from 11? Comment on other sound effects in the line.

5.   By comparison with Aeneas' descent into Hades in *Aeneid* VI, Orpheus' journey seems to have been accomplished with lightning-fast speed; how does the meter in 14–15 help convey this impression?

          inamoenaque . . . dominum (16): an epic periphrasis for Pluto, lord of the dead.

16   **umbrārum dominum**: a highly effective enjambement, punctuated by caesura and intensified by the roaring **r**'s and the foreboding assonance of **um-/-um/-um** (under the ictus in each of the first three feet).

    ***pellō, pellere, pepulī, pulsus**, *to beat against, strike; to drive away, banish, expel*.

          pulsīsque ad carmina nervīs: *with the strings* (of his lyre) *strummed to accompany his song*; Orpheus does not merely address the prince of darkness and his bride, but tries to charm them through the magic of his lyrics. Cf. **nervōsque ad verba moventem** (40), which precisely balances the phrase here and with it frames the entire song (17–39).

17   **sīc ait**: the enjambement and diaeresis effectively introduce Orpheus' lengthy song.
    nūmina: voc., with the gen. phrase **positī . . . mundī**; note the soundplay with **carmina** (identically positioned in 16) and **mundī**.
    mundus, -ī, m., *world, universe*.

18   **reccidō, reccidere, reccidī, reccāsūrus**, *to fall back, sink back* (here pres. tense).
    *****quisquis, quidquid**, indefinite rel. pron., *any who, whoever, whatever*.
        quidquid . . . creāmur: "we," the subject of **reccidimus**, is the antecedent; the n. sing. pron. is used here for a generalizing effect, *whichever of us are created mortal*.
    mortālis, -is, -e, *subject to death, mortal*.
    creō, -āre, -āvī, -ātus, *to beget, create*.

19   **sī licet et . . . sinitis** (20): the protasis of a simple fact condition, with **dēscendī** (21) the verb of the apodosis.
    *****falsus, -a, -um**, *untrue, false; misleading, deceptive*.
        falsī . . . ōris: the beguiling singer here promises to utter only the truth (whether he does or not is a matter of interpretation).
    positīs: = **dēpositīs**, *set aside*; the implication is that he sometimes does, or at least can, speak evasively or obscurely.
    ambāgēs, -um, f. pl., *a circuitous path; long-winded, obscure*, or *evasive speech*.

20   *****opācus, -a, -um**, *shaded; shadowy, dark, dim*.

21   **Tartara, -ōrum**, n. pl., *Tartarus* (the Underworld).
    utī: = **ut**.
    villōsus, -a, -um, *shaggy, hairy*.
        villōsa . . . / terna . . . guttura (22): note the elaborate interlocked word order, producing with **Medūsaeī . . . mōnstrī** a brilliant golden line.
    colubra, -ae, f., *serpent, snake* (used especially of the "hair" of monsters, as here with **villōsa**, *bristling with serpents*).

22   **ternī, -ae, -a**, pl. adj., *three (each), three at a time, three in succession*.
    Medūsaeus, -a, -um, *of Medusa* (the Gorgon whose hair consisted of living serpents); (here) *resembling Medusa, Medusa-like*.
        Medūsaeī . . . mōnstrī: Cerberus, the three-headed watchdog of the Underworld, was born of the snake-demon Echidna, a sister of Medusa; like Medusa, he had snaky locks and was so hideous that a single glance at him could turn a man to stone (cf. 65–66).
    vinciō, vincīre, vīnxī, vīnctus, *to bind, tie up*.
    guttur, gutturis, n., *throat*.
    mōnstrum, -ī, n., *omen, portent; monster*.

23   **causa . . . coniūnx**: an abrupt formulation; note the harsh alliteration of c, continued in **calcāta**.
    calcō, -āre, -āvī, -ātus, *to trample; to tread, step on*.
    venēnum, -ī, n., *a potent herb; poison, venom*.

24   **vīpera, -ae**, f., *viper, serpent*.

sīc ait: "Ō positī sub terrā nūmina mundī,
in quem reccidimus, quidquid mortāle creāmur,
sī licet et falsī positīs ambāgibus ōris
20 vēra loquī sinitis, nōn hūc, ut opāca vidērem
Tartara, dēscendī, nec utī villōsa colubrīs
terna Medūsaeī vincīrem guttura mōnstrī;
causa viae est coniūnx, in quam calcāta venēnum
vīpera diffūdit crēscentēsque abstulit annōs.
25 Posse patī voluī nec mē temptāsse negābō;

Discussion Questions

1. In what respects does the expression **falsī positīs ambāgibus ōris / vēra loquī** (19–20) seem redundant? What might Ovid's purpose be in having Orpheus speak this way?

2. What is the point of having Orpheus mention two purposes that did *not* motivate his descent into the underworld (20–22)?

3. How is the intricate interweaving of the three adjectives and three nouns in 21–22 (**villōsa . . . mōnstrī**) neatly suited to Ovid's depiction of the hellhound Cerberus?

diffundō, diffundere, diffūdī, diffūsus, *to pour widely; to pour into, diffuse.*

crēscentēs annōs: *her budding years* (we might say, *in the bloom of youth*); cf. **iūstōs . . . annōs** (36).

25 **Posse . . . temptāsse**: note the striking **p/t** alliteration and the assonance of **-osse/-āsse**.

patī: complementary infin. with **posse**, *to endure* (i.e., his loss).

nec mē temptāsse negābō: *nor shall I deny that I tried* (to endure). Both the verb (**temptāsse = temptāvisse**) and the curious double negative recall **nē nōn temptāret et umbrās** (12); each phrase follows a reference to the serpent's strike and Orpheus' mourning.

26   **vīcit Amor**: sc. **mē**; asyndeton (we expect **sed** or **autem**) and the very brevity of the sentence underscore Orpheus' point (cf. the expanded **vōs quoque iūnxit Amor** 29).

      Superā . . . ōra: cf. **superās . . . aurās** (11).

27   **an sit**: sc. **bene nōtus**; the series of monosyllables, and the consequent jerkiness of the dactylic rhythm, both preceding and following **dubitō**, help suggest Orpheus' initial hesitancy (or the hesitancy he feigns).

      et: = **etiam**; the anaphora of **et hīc** strengthens the equation Orpheus makes between Love's two victories in 26 and 29.

      auguror, augurārī, augurātus sum, *to foretell by augury; to intuit, sense, surmise.*

      esse: i.e., **eum (Amōrem) esse nōtum**, indirect statement with **auguror**.

28   *****fāma, -ae**, f., *news, report; tradition, story.*

      veteris . . . rapīnae: i.e., Pluto's rape of Persephone (which Ovid himself had included in *Met.* V, in a tale narrated by Orpheus' own mother, the Muse Calliope).

      mentior, mentīrī, mentītus sum, *to lie; to invent, fabricate.*

29   **Per**: with oaths, *by.*

         Per . . . loca . . . / per Chaos (30): anaphora and asyndeton lend intensity to Orpheus' oath, as do the strong epithets (**plēna timōris, ingēns, vāstī**—these last two effectively juxtaposed). Cf. **in loca plēna metūs** (IV.111 above).

      ego: in prose this word (subject of **ōrō** 31) would either precede or follow the prepositional phrases; but in oaths Ovid favors this arrangement, which emphasizes the subject.

30   **Chaos, -ī**, n., *Chaos* (the formless state of the universe before creation); *the Underworld.*

      vāstus, -a, -um, *desolate, lifeless; huge, immense.*

      silentia: poetic pl.; cf. 53 below.

31   *****Eurydicē, Eurydicēs**, acc. **Eurydicēn**, f., *Eurydice* (a Thracian nymph, wife of Orpheus—for the delay of her name to this late point in the narrative, see above on **quam** 11, and for the Greek case endings cf. **Daphnē** and **Thisbē**).

      properāta . . . fāta: *premature death*; note the assonance.

      retexō, retexere, retexuī, retextus, *to unweave* (Ovid has in mind the myth of the Fates, or Parcae, weaving the tapestry of a person's life from birth to death).

      *****fātum, -ī**, n., *prophecy; destiny, fate; Fate* (as a deity); *doom, death* (often pl. for sing.).

34   **Tendimus . . . vōsque**: note the **hūc/haec** anaphora, the parallel placement of **omnēs** and **ultima**, and the emphatic **vōsque** (and cf. **vōs** 29, **vōbīs** 32, **vestrī** 37).

35   **longissima rēgna**: poetic pl., *the most enduring dominion over* (with the objective gen. **generis**).

      tenētis: note the wordplay with this verb at the end of the sentence and the assonant **tendimus** at the beginning.

vīcit Amor. Superā deus hic bene nōtus in ōrā est;
an sit et hīc, dubitō. Sed et hīc tamen auguror esse,
fāmaque sī veteris nōn est mentīta rapīnae,
vōs quoque iūnxit Amor. Per ego haec loca plēna timōris,
30   per Chaos hoc ingēns vāstīque silentia rēgnī,
Eurydicēs, ōrō, properāta retexite fāta!
Omnia dēbentur vōbīs, paulumque morātī
sērius aut citius sēdem properāmus ad ūnam.
Tendimus hūc omnēs, haec est domus ultima, vōsque
35   hūmānī generis longissima rēgna tenētis.
Haec quoque, cum iūstōs mātūra perēgerit annōs,

Discussion Questions

1.   In view of its context, what do you suppose is the intended effect of the poetic plural **silentia** (30)?

2.   Some readers take **properāta retexite fāta** (31) to mean *reweave Eurydice's destiny, too swiftly ended* rather than *unweave her premature death*; which makes better sense in this context and why?

3.   Comment on the placement of **omnia** and **ūnam** (32–33); what is the intended effect and how is the idea continued in the next verse?

---

36   **Haec**: i.e., Eurydice, but the word continues the anaphora with **hūc** and **haec** in 34.
       iūstus, -a, -um, *lawful, legitimate; rightful, proper, deserved.*
       mātūrus, -a, -um, *ripe; advanced in age.*
    *peragō, peragere, perēgī, perāctus, *to chase; to complete; to go through* (space or time); *to live out, complete* (a period of time).

37 iūris . . . vestrī: *under your authority* (a variety of possessive gen.).
   *mūnus, mūneris, n., *a required task; tribute, offering* (to a deity); *gift* (with prō, *as a gift*); *favor, service.*
   *ūsus, -ūs, m., *use, employment; the right to use* or *enjoy* (especially with reference to property owned by another); *potential for use, utility; marriage* (one type of Roman civil marriage, which became binding following a full year of cohabitation).
38 Quod: here, *but.*
   *venia, -ae, f., *favor, kindness, blessing* (especially in a religious sense); *forgiveness, pardon; reprieve, remission.*
   certum est / . . . mihī (39): *I am determined* (lit., *it is a certainty for me*) + infin.; mihī is delayed to balance coniuge.
39 nōlle: essentially equivalent to nōn here, but with greater force.
   lētō gaudēte duōrum: the t/d alliteration, the assonance of lēt-/-dēt-, the accented ō's, and the abrupt imperative add a harsh, melancholy tone to the song's close.
40 Tālia . . . moventem: this line corresponds precisely to pulsīsque . . . / sīc ait (16–17) and with it provides a chiastic frame for Orpheus' song; the internal rhyme in dīcentem . . . moventem adds an aptly musical sound effect. With the participles sc. Orpheum, object of flēbant (41).
41 exsanguis, -is, -e, *bloodless; pale; lifeless.*
   *fleō, flēre, flēvī, flētus, *to weep, cry; to weep for, lament.*
   Tantalus, -ī, m., *Tantalus* (a Lydian king, son of Zeus and father of Pelops).
      Tantalus . . . refugam (42): like the others named in the next few lines (and described by Ovid earlier in *Met.* IV), Tantalus had committed a crime that earned him eternal torment in Hades. Since Tantalus' offense was culinary (he had butchered his son and served him to the gods in a stew to test their omniscience), he was cursed with perpetual hunger and thirst, standing beneath a tree whose fruits remained just beyond his reach and in a stream whose waters receded from his lips whenever he sought to drink. Here, stunned by Orpheus' song, each of these shades momentarily ceases from its labors.
42 captāvit: here, with nec Tantalus, *and Tantalus did not try to seize* (or *catch at*).
   refugus, -a, -um, *fleeting; receding.*
   stupuitque Ixīonis orbis: *and Ixion's wheel, in amazement, ceased to turn*; Orpheus' song was powerful enough to mesmerize, not only men and beasts (like the volucrēs in 43), but even inanimate objects.
   Ixīōn, Ixīonis, m., *Ixion* (king of the Lapiths, who was tied to a perpetually turning wheel in Hades as punishment for his attempt to seduce Juno).
43 *carpō, carpere, carpsī, carptus, *to pluck, gather; to tear at; to travel, pursue* (a path).
      carpsēre . . . volucrēs: the allusion is to the giant Tityus, who, for his attempted rape of Leto, was tied down to several acres of ground in the Underworld and exposed to vultures that tore constantly at his liver (the organ thought to be the source of the libido and other passions);

iūris erit vestrī—prō mūnere poscimus ūsum.
Quod sī Fāta negant veniam prō coniuge, certum est
nōlle redīre mihī; lētō gaudēte duōrum."
40   Tālia dīcentem nervōsque ad verba moventem
exsanguēs flēbant animae; nec Tantalus undam
captāvit refugam, stupuitque Ixīonis orbis,
nec carpsēre iecur volucrēs, urnīsque vacārunt

Discussion Questions

1. What rhetorical effect does Ovid hope to achieve by his repeated use of the second person pronoun in 29–37?

2. One argument for releasing Eurydice (25–29) precedes Orpheus' oath and entreaty in 29–31, and another (32–37) follows; what are the arguments and which is stronger? How economically is the second point made, and how does this economy (or the lack of it) coincide with Orpheus' promise in **positīs ambāgibus** (19)? At what point earlier in Orpheus' speech is the second argument anticipated?

3. What tone is established through the use of the words **iūstōs, iūris,** and **poscimus ūsum** (36–37)? What impression of Orpheus' attitude toward his spouse may this language be intended to convey?

4. How does Ovid carefully position his words to accentuate the internal rhyme in 40?

---

carpsēre = carpsērunt.
iecur, iecoris, n., *the liver.*
*volucris, volucris,** f., *a winged creature, bird.*
urnīs . . . / Bēlides (44): 49 of the 50 Danaids (daughters of the Libyan king Danaus, son of king Belus), in obedience to their father, murdered their bridegroom-cousins on their wedding night and were punished in Hades by having to fill with water urns that perpetually leaked.
*vacō, -āre, -āvī, -ātus,** *to be empty, unfilled; to be free from, take a rest from* (**vacārunt = vacāvērunt**).

44 **Bēlis, Bēlidos**, nom. pl. **Bēlides**, f., *descendants of Belus* (the **-is, -idos** endings are a common patronymic formation), *the Danaids*.

Sīsyphus, -ī, m., *Sisyphus* (this king of Corinth had offended both Zeus and Pluto and was condemned in Hades to push a huge stone up a hill, only to have it roll back down again each time he neared the top; the apostrophe here enlivens the narrative).

*saxum, -ī, n., *a stone, rock, boulder*.

45 **Tunc . . . genās** (46): the clause is an indirect statement following **fāma est**, *there is a story that* or *it is said that*; the prose word order would be **Fāma est genās Eumenidum, carmine victārum, tunc prīmum lacrimīs maduisse.**

46 **Eumenis, Eumenidos**, gen. pl. **Eumenidum**, f. (usually pl.), *one of the Eumenides* or *Furies* (goddesses of vengeance, who were generally severe and implacable).

madēscō, madēscere, maduī, *to become wet*.

gena, -ae, f., *the side of the face, cheek*; pl., the area around the eyes, *the eyes*.

rēgius, -a, -um, *of the king, royal*.

47 **ōrantī**: sc. **Orpheō**, indirect object with **negāre**, *to say no to* (complementary infin. with **sustinet**).

quī regit īma: i.e., Pluto, subject (with **rēgia coniūnx** = Persephone) of **sustinet**.

49 **inter . . . tardō**: the anastrophe and enjambement of **inter** (which in prose would precede its object **umbrās**), with the off-beat caesura and **et** following, the three spondees and conflict of ictus and accent in **incessit passū**, and the harsh alliteration of **t**, all sound out the slow, limping cadence of Eurydice's gait.

incessit: this verb is often used of the slow, orderly movement of a person of stately, even majestic bearing; there is perhaps that nuance here: Eurydice steps slowly, serenely, not just because of her wound, but also as befits the ghostly spectre of a river nymph.

dē vulnere: Eurydice still feels the effects of the snakebite because she is among the recently deceased (**umbrās . . . recentēs** 48).

tardō: with **passū** (not **vulnere**), abl. of manner.

50 **Hanc . . . et lēgem . . . accipit**: **hanc** = Eurydice; the zeugma (Orpheus *received* his wife and *accepted* the condition that Pluto and Persephone imposed) is perhaps meant as a further depersonalizing effect.

lēgem: the *restriction* is explained in the following jussive noun clause (an indirect command).

Rhodopēius . . . hērōs: some manuscripts have **Orpheus** instead of **hērōs**, but with the epithet **Rhodopēius** the name is a redundancy and the reading adopted here is comparable with **Rhodopēius . . . vātēs** (11–12 above) and **Paphius . . . hērōs** (X.290 below).

*hērōs, hērōos, m., *hero* (another Greek formation).

51 **retrō**: i.e., back down into the Underworld; this condition may recall for readers the biblical story of Lot in Sodom and Gomorrah.

Bēlides, inque tuō sēdistī, Sīsyphe, saxō.
45 Tunc prīmum lacrimīs victārum carmine fāma est
Eumenidum maduisse genās; nec rēgia coniūnx
sustinet ōrantī nec quī regit īma negāre,
Eurydicēnque vocant. Umbrās erat illa recentēs
inter, et incessit passū dē vulnere tardō.
50 Hanc simul et lēgem Rhodopēius accipit hērōs,
nē flectat retrō sua lūmina, dōnec Avernās
exierit vallēs, aut irrita dōna futūra.
Carpitur acclīvis per mūta silentia trāmes,

Discussion Questions

1. What seem to you the most striking sound effects in 43–44?

2. What is your reaction to the picture of Sisyphus presented in 44? How does this color your interpretation of the narrative's overall tone and purpose?

3. What consonant sound predominates in Ovid's description of the Furies (45–46) and what is the effect?

4. Comment on the word-picture in **Umbrās . . . illa recentēs** (48).

---

*lūmen, lūminis, n., *light; an eye* (especially pl.); *vision, gaze, glance* (sing. or pl.).
dōnec, conj., *until.*
Avernus, -a, -um, *of the Underworld, infernal.*
52 vallēs, vallis, f., *valley* or, with reference to Hades, *the abyss.*
irritus, -a, -um, *nullified, void.*
> irrita dōna futūra: = dōna futūra esse irrita, indirect statement after the implied speech word in **lēgem.**
dōna: pl. for sing., i.e., the gift of Eurydice's resurrection from the dead.
53 Carpitur . . . trāmes: English would use an active construction, *they pressed their way along the upward sloping path.*
acclīvis, -is, -e, *inclined, sloping upwards.*
> acclīvis . . . opācā (54): the numerous epithets and asyndeton counterbalance the brevity of Ovid's narration of the trek to upper earth.
mūtus, -a, -um, *mute, soundless, speechless.*
trāmes, trāmitis, m., *footpath, trail.*

54 **cālīgō, cālīginis,** f., *darkness; gloom.*
   ***dēnsus, -a, -um,** thick, dense; frequent.*
55 ***margō, marginis,** m., wall; border, edge; margin.*
56 **dēficiō, dēficere, dēfēcī, dēfectus,** *to fail; to lose strength, collapse, faint.*
   nē dēficeret: the understood subject of the (positive) fear clause is
      Eurydice.
   nē dēficeret metuēns avidusque videndī: note the effective chiasmus
      and the soundplay in **avidus . . . videndī;** both epithets modify the
      subject **amāns** (57), *the lover* (i.e., Orpheus).
   ***metuō, metuere, metuī, metūtus,** to fear, be afraid of.*
   avidus, -a, -um, *greedy; desirous (of), eager (for)* + gen.
   videndī: sc. **eam,** i.e., Eurydice.
57 **flexit amāns . . . illa relāpsa est:** chiasmus, with the verbs framing the line.
   relābor, relābī, relāpsus sum, *to fall* or *slip backward.*
58 **bracchiaque . . . certāns:** the cacophonous alliteration of **r, c/q,** and **t/d,** the
      series of spondees, elisions, and conflict of ictus and accent following the
      opening dactyl, the anaphora and assonance in the four verbals (each
      describing intense or violent action), and the division of the verse by the
      carefully positioned participles (the first at the caesura, the second at line's
      end), all contribute to the "soundtrack," as Eurydice starts to slip backward
      into the abyss and desperately thrashes out her arms toward Orpheus.
   intendō, intendere, intendī, intentus, *to stretch; to stretch forth, hold out.*
      intendēns . . . certāns: these participles are taken by most editors to
         describe Orpheus, since he is assumed to be the subject in the next
         verse (see on **cēdentēs . . . aurās**), but 58–59 more likely refer to
         Eurydice for several reasons: the clauses immediately preceding and
         following both refer to Eurydice; the actions in 58, especially the
         priority given to the passive **prēndī,** and the violent **arripit** in 59,
         seem more naturally attributed to her as she slips and falls; **īnfēlīx** (59)
         is deliberately repeated in **īnfēlīx Lēthaea** (70), a reference to
         Eurydice's counterpart, not Orpheus', in the simile of 68–71; and
         finally, the contrast between Eurydice's valiant struggle and her
         husband's relative ineptitude further diminishes the hero's image, in
         keeping with Ovid's parodying intentions.
   ***prēndō, prēndere, prēndī, prēnsus,** to grasp, seize, take hold of; to catch,
      capture.*
   certō, -āre, -āvī, -ātus, *to contend, strive, struggle.*
59 **cēdentēs . . . aurās:** *the retreating air* (of the world of the living); for **aurae**
      in this fairly common sense, cf. *Met.* IV.478. As Eurydice reaches out for
      Orpheus, she catches hold of nothing but the longed-for air of upper earth,
      which they had very nearly reached (55) but which now retreats from her
      outstretched arms as she falls backward. Most readers, comparing (among
      other examples) the scene in *Aen.* II.791–94, where Aeneas grasps only a
      wisp of air as he tries to embrace Creusa's ghost, refer **īnfēlīx arripit** to
      Orpheus and **aurās** to Eurydice's shade (a possible interpretation, but see

arduus, obscūrus, cālīgine dēnsus opācā.
55 Nec procul āfuerant tellūris margine summae;
hīc, nē dēficeret metuēns avidusque videndī,
flexit amāns oculōs. Et prōtinus illa relāpsa est,
bracchiaque intendēns, prēndīque et prēndere certāns,
nīl nisi cēdentēs īnfēlīx arripit aurās;
60 iamque iterum moriēns, nōn est dē coniuge quicquam
questa suō (quid enim nisi sē quererētur amātam?),
suprēmumque "Valē," quod iam vīx auribus ille

Discussion Questions

1. What is the intended effect of the chiasmus in 56?

2. How are the meter, the elision, and the chiasmus in 57 especially appropriate
   to the sense?

---

above on 58 and note also that in *Aen.* II.772 Creusa, not Aeneas, is
described as **īnfēlīx**).
arripiō, arripere, arripuī, arreptus, *to grasp, take hold of, embrace.*
60 **est . . . / questa** (61): Eurydice is subject.
quicquam, adv., *in any respect, at all.*
61 **quid . . . amātam**: **sē . . . amātam** (esse) is indirect statement after the
potential subjunctive **quererētur**, *for what could she complain of except
that she had been loved.*
62 **suprēmum**: n. acc., modifying the word **valē**, which as Eurydice's final
utterance is object of **dīxit** (63). Only that last fleeting word falls into a
quick dactyl—the rest of the line is in an aptly spondaic and, with the
series of monosyllables, halting rhythm.

63   **acciperet**: subjn. in a rel. clause of characteristic, perhaps with the force of result (her cry was so quick and faint that Orpheus could barely hear it).

         revolvō, revolvere, revoluī, revolūtus, *to roll back, return*; pass., *to fall back again* (cf. **relāpsa est** 57—there she first slips and now she tumbles quickly backward).

         eōdem, adv., *to* or *into the same place* (the redundancy in **re-** and the adverbs **rūrsus** and **eōdem** are deliberately emphatic—and cf. **iterum** 60 and **geminā** 64).

64   **Nōn aliter stupuit . . . / quam . . . quī** (65) **. . . / quam quī . . .** (68) **. . . tūque** (69): momentarily the hero *was paralyzed* with horror; the quick dactyls in 64–65 suggest how suddenly this happened. In his inability to act or speak, Orpheus is compared in this double simile with characters who were turned to stone in two otherwise unattested transformation tales; for **nōn aliter quam,** cf. IV.122 above.

         geminā nece: abl. of cause; cf. **iterum moriēns** (60) and **geminī . . . cruōris** (IV.161).

         Orpheus, -ī, m., *Orpheus* (the hero is at last named; -eu- in the nom. case here is a diphthong).

65   **tria . . . / colla canis** (66): the tale's second reference to Cerberus (cf. **terna . . . guttura mōnstrī** 22).

         quī timidus: with **vīdit**; in prose the words would follow **quam**. The character (whose name is unknown) apparently gazed upon Cerberus as Hercules was leading him on a chain leash to king Eurystheus and, paralyzed by fear, was turned to stone.

         mediō: sc. **collō**.

         catēna, -ae, f., *a chain*; pl., *chains, fetters*.

66   **quem . . . prior** (67): the full expression here would be **quem pavor nōn relīquit, antequam nātūra prior relīquit**; in English we would say, *who did not lose his fear until he lost his original nature,* i.e., as a human being.

         pavor, pavōris, m., *sudden fear, terror*.

         antequam or (by tmesis) **ante . . . quam,** conj., *before*.

67   **oborior, oborīrī, obortus sum,** *to rise up, spring up*.

68   **quam quī . . . / Ōlenos** (69): i.e., **aut quam Ōlenos, quī . . . trāxit**; most manuscripts read **quīque,** but (as Anderson notes) **quam quī** more clearly introduces the second simile in parallel with the first (cf. **quam . . . quī** 65). We can only deduce from the context, and roughly comparable tales, that Lethaea had offended some deity, apparently in boasting of her own beauty, and when her lover (or spouse) Olenos attempted to accept both the blame and the punishment in her place, the two were transformed to stone.

69   **Ōlenos, -ī,** m., *Olenos* (the character is otherwise unknown, but there are several Greek towns with this name—and Herodotus 4.35 mentions an early Greek named Olen who, like Orpheus, was a minstrel and composer of hymns).

         nocēns: here, *guilty*; note the assonance in **Ōlenos esse nocēns**.

         tūque: with **quam** (68), i.e., *than Olenos . . . and you, oh Lethaea*; for the

acciperet, dīxit, revolūtaque rūrsus eōdem est.
    Nōn aliter stupuit geminā nece coniugis Orpheus,
65   quam tria quī timidus, mediō portante catēnās,
colla canis vīdit, quem nōn pavor ante relīquit,
quam nātūra prior, saxō per corpus obortō;
quam quī in sē crīmen trāxit voluitque vidērī
Olenos esse nocēns, tūque, ō cōnfīsa figūrae
70   īnfēlīx Lēthaea tuae, iūnctissima quondam
pectora, nunc lapidēs, quōs ūmida sustinet Īdē.

Discussion Question

1.   Contrast the meter of 63 with that of 62; in what way is the shift appropriate?

2.   What are the several points of correspondence between the circumstances of
Orpheus and Eurydice and those of the characters in the two similes (64–71)?
Are the similes an effective part of the narrative, or do you find them unduly
digressive?—defend your response.

---

dramatic apostrophe, cf. **Sīsyphe** (44).

cōnfīdō, cōnfīdere, cōnfīdī, cōnfīsus + dat., *to trust in, have confidence in,
be sure of.*

    cōnfīsa figūrae . . . tuae: *so self-assured in your beauty;* note the
    alliteration with **īnfēlīx.**

70   **īnfēlīx Lēthaea:** enjambement underscores the epithet and draws our attention
back to **īnfēlīx** (Eurydice) in 59; both women were young (presumably) and
beautiful, and had lovers who hoped to rescue them from death.

Lēthaea, -ae, f., *Lethaea* (the character is not otherwise known, but the
name, like the adj. **Lēthaeus, -a, -um,** is doubtless meant to recall Lethe,
the River of Forgetfulness in the Underworld, and all of its dark, infernal
associations).

iūnctissima quondam / pectora, nunc lapidēs (71): both phrases, linked by
the antithetical *then/now* adverbs (and the **iūnc-/nunc** assonance), are in
apposition with **Olenos** and **Lēthaea.**

71   **ūmidus, -a, -um,** *wet, moist; rainy.*

sustinet: here, simply *holds* (i.e., the rocks, boulders perhaps, were situated
on the mountain).

Īdē, Īdēs, f., *Mt. Ida* (there were mountains of this name in both Crete and
Troy—probably Ovid means the latter, site of the judgment of Paris and
described by Horace, *Carm.* III.20.16, as **aquōsa**).

72 **Ōrantem . . . volentem**: sc. **eum** (Orpheus); the participles, both objects of **arcuerat** (73) and both to be taken with the adv. **frūstrā**, effectively frame the line.

73 **portitor, portitōris**, m., *tollkeeper* (one who collects import or export taxes); as applied to Charon (who collected pennies from the tongues of the dead before allowing them to cross over the Styx into Hades), *ferryman*.
  arceō, arcēre, arcuī, *to contain, restrain; to keep away, drive back*.
  Septem . . . diēbus: abl. of duration of time, instead of the much commoner acc. construction.

74 **squālidus, -a, -um**, *rough; filthy, unbathed, unkempt*.
  rīpa, -ae, f., *bank* (of a river, here the Styx).
  *****Cerēs, Cereris**, f., *Ceres* (goddess of grain, identified with the Greek Demeter, mother of Persephone/Proserpina).
   Cereris sine mūnere: Orpheus is *without Ceres' gift* (of grain), first because he refuses to eat (just as he refuses to bathe) and also perhaps because Ceres, as Persephone's mother, will not aid in his further assault on her daughter's realm.

75 **alimentum, -ī**, n., *food*; pl., *nourishment, sustenance* (here predicate nom. with **fuēre** = **fuērunt**).

76 **Esse . . . crūdēlēs**: the prose order would be **deōs Erebī esse crūdēlēs**, indirect statement after **questus** (*complaining that*).
  Erebus, -ī, m., *Erebus* (son of Chaos, father of Charon, and god of darkness); *the Underworld*.

77 **Rhodopē, Rhodopēs**, acc. **Rhodopēn**, f., *Mt. Rhodope* (see on **Rhodopēius** 11).
   Rhodopēn pulsumque aquilōnibus Haemum: the harsh p/q alliteration, the booming assonance of **-um** (under the ictus in **pulsum**), and the hissing s's are perhaps intended to suggest the storming of the wild north winds as Orpheus retreats from Hades, and indeed from civilization itself, here at the close of the tale.
  aquilō, aquilōnis, m., *the north wind*.
  Haemus, -ī, m., *Haemus* (another mountain in northern Thrace).

And then he struck from forth the strings a sound
Of deep and fearful melody. Alas!
In times long past, when fair Eurydice
With her bright eyes sat listening by his side,
He gently sang of high and heavenly themes.

From "Orpheus," Percy Bysshe Shelley, 1820

Ōrantem frūstrāque iterum trānsīre volentem
portitor arcuerat. Septem tamen ille diēbus
squālidus in rīpā Cereris sine mūnere sēdit;
75 cūra dolorque animī lacrimaeque alimenta fuēre.
Esse deōs Erebī crūdēlēs questus, in altam
sē recipit Rhodopēn pulsumque aquilōnibus Haemum.

Discussion Questions

1. Comment on the combined effects of sound, meter, and polysyndeton in 75.

2. Orpheus' actions at the very end of the tale (76–77) do not coincide with what he had pledged he would do in the end of his song to Pluto and Persephone. What do you make of the discrepancy? Compare Pyramus' pledge and his actions in IV.108–21 and Thisbe's words and deeds in 151–63 with Orpheus' actions here. In view of the burlesque elements that appear at least occasionally in the story, what overall response to the tale do you suppose Ovid expected of his readers? What is your own response?

Hermes, Eurydice, and Orpheus, 5th century B.C. relief
Museo Archeologico Nazionale, Naples

PYGMALION

Metamorphoses X.238–97

From the beginning of time it would seem, at least from the male perspective, man has quested for, and even sought to create, the perfect woman. Robotics produced *The Stepford Wives*, Frankenstein stitched together a bride for his monster, and Professor Henry Higgins fashioned his "fair lady" from the raggedy flower girl, Liza Doolittle, in Lerner and Loewe's delightful musical, an adaptation from George Bernard Shaw's *Pygmalion*. But Ovid, Shaw's own ultimate inspiration and our principal ancient literary source for the tale, has provided us with a far more miraculous transformation. Offended by the profligacy of the daughters of Propoetus (who, for their impiety, were transformed by Venus into prostitutes and then hardened into stone), the Cypriote sculptor Pygmalion withdrew from all contact with women, living the life of a celibate and dedicating himself wholly to his art. Eventually he sculpted an ivory statue of a maiden more beautiful than any ever born, and then promptly fell in love with his own creation. The central panel of Ovid's narrative focuses in detail on the artist's elegiac (and to some extent ritualistic) courtship of his ivory maiden and then, when the festival of Venus had arrived, on his prayer to the goddess that his own wife might be, if not the statue itself, then at least a woman in her likeness. In return for his piety, Venus grants Pygmalion's wish, reversing both the process by which she had transformed the impious Propoetides and the usual (human to sub-human) direction of metamorphosis in Ovid's poem: as the sculptor kisses his "Sleeping Beauty," her skin grows warm and soft, her veins begin to pulse, a blush comes to her face (unlike the bloodless, shameless Propoetides), and she raises up her eyes to glimpse at once the light of heaven and her lover's gaze. Despite the unnatural inception of their affair, and under the benign guidance of Venus, the two are wed and soon have a daughter, Paphos, who (in an etiological aspect of the myth) gave her name to a city of Cyprus famous for its cult of the goddess.

It is little wonder that a story with these fairy-tale qualities, so sensuous and sentimental, and so focused on artistic creation, should have inspired, not only the talents of George Bernard Shaw, and Lerner and Loewe, but such artists (among many, many others) as Falconet, Rodin, and Gerome, whose own creations are pictured in the pages that follow. "Fellow-artists," one ought to say—for it was very much Ovid's point that we should see Pygmalion, not merely as a man, but as a creative genius. In this role, Pygmalion shares certain qualities with Orpheus, which the reader is invited to explore, even as his ivory maiden has much in common with Ovid's Eurydice. To note only an obvious point or two, both men attempt to use their artistic talents to control their women: the one fails, despite the magical charm of his music, to restore his spouse to life; the other succeeds, through piety and the power of art, in bringing his ideal woman to life. The wives themselves are one-dimensional, manipulated: Eurydice's role is but to die, and die again, uttering only an uncomplaining "farewell"; the ivory maiden, who speaks not even a single word and has no name (though in postclassical adaptations she is called Galatea), is shaped, and handled, and, when brought to life, gazes heavenward at her creator as at a god.

With these points in mind, along with the condemning attitudes about the virtue and beauty of "real" women that are expressed early in the narrative, some readers view Pygmalion in a negative light, as an eccentric misogynist and a manipulator. But the story's misogyny is perhaps better attributed to the persona of its narrator, Orpheus himself, who in mourning the death of Eurydice has gone on to reject all other women and is here singing (hence the quotation marks enclosing the text below) one of a series of ballads protesting their vile and illicit loves. Pygmalion's religious devotion to Venus is remarkable, as can be seen from her extraordinary intervention on his behalf, and, in the intensity of his reverence for his beloved, he is certainly nearer to Pyramus than to Ovid's Apollo or even to Orpheus: in the end, it may be that the poet expects us to fault Pygmalion for nothing more than the extremity of his idealism.

In his role as artist in fact, and in particular as an artist of the erotic, Pygmalion has much in common with Ovid himself. Both the poet and Pygmalion (who is at once a creator and the poet's own creation) revere love, and beauty, and the illusion of reality. It has been observed that Ovid's comment on the realism of Pygmalion's statue—*ars adeō latet arte suā* ("so utterly was his artifice concealed by his art")—might well serve as a prime tenet of the poet's own philosophy of art.

"Pygmalion and Galatea"
Auguste Rodin, 1889
Metropolitan Museum of Art
New York

238 **Sunt . . . ausae:** the opening line is neatly symmetrical, with **Venerem** at the axis, surrounded by **obscēnae . . . Prōpoetides,** and verbals framing the whole; the sentence's prose order would be **Tamen Prōpoetides obscēnae ausae sunt negāre Venerem esse deam.**

tamen: i.e., ignoring the fate of their compatriots, the Cerastae, whom Venus had transformed into bulls for butchering their guests—a story told by Ovid in the preceding passage.

obscēnus, -a, -um, *ill-omened; filthy, loathsome; lewd.*

   obscēnae . . . ausae: Ovid likes to arrange pairs of end-rhyming and grammatically connected words such as these two by setting one at the caesura, with the last syllable under the ictus, and the other at line's end; the effect is to accentuate both the connection and the assonance (cf. I.460 above).

Prōpoetides, Prōpoetidum, f. pl., *the Propoetides* (daughters of Propoetus of Cyprus, who were, according to this legend, the first prostitutes).

239 **prō quō:** i.e., *for this offense.*

sua . . . / corpora cum fōrmā (240): a kind of hendiadys; we would say simply *their beautiful bodies.*

īrā: abl. of cause.

240 **prīmae . . . feruntur:** sc. **esse,** *they are said to be the first.*

vulgō, -āre, -āvī, -ātus, *to make available to the masses; to prostitute* (**vulgāsse** = **vulgāvisse**).

241 *****pudor, pudōris,** m., *sense of shame; decency, chastity.*

sanquisque indūruit ōris: Ovid imaginatively blends the physiological with the psychological—when we are ashamed, blood rushes to our faces and we blush, but when we cease to feel shame and to blush, it is because the blood has hardened in our veins.

indūrēscō, indūrēscere, indūruī, *to grow hard, harden, set.*

242 **rigidus, -a, -um,** *rigid, stiff; unyielding.*

parvō . . . discrīmine: *with little noticeable change,* i.e., from their former nature as "hardened" prostitutes; abl. of attendant circumstance.

*****silex, silicis,** m., *hard stone, flint* (often used of the absence of emotions, or "hard-heartedness," in persons—cf. *Am.* I.11.9 below).

versae: sc. **sunt.**

243 **Quās:** = **Eās** (with **agentīs**).

quia, conj., *since, because.*

*****Pygmaliōn, Pygmaliōnis,** m., *Pygmalion* (legendary king of Cyprus, though here seen only as a sculptor).

aevum, -ī, n., *time, age;* **aevum agere,** idiom, *to spend one's life, live.*

per crīmen: here, *in wickedness, viciously.*

244 **offēnsus, -a, -um,** *offended, shocked.*

vitiīs, quae plūrima: English would take the adjective with the noun rather than the pron., *the countless vices which . . . .*

245 **sine coniuge caelebs / vīvēbat . . . cōnsorte carēbat** (246): the second clause intensifies the first; note the harsh c alliteration at the end of both verses, and the framing of 246 with the assonant imperfect tense verbs.

"Sunt tamen obscēnae Venerem Prōpoetides ausae
esse negāre deam; prō quō sua, nūminis īrā,
240   corpora cum fōrmā prīmae vulgāsse feruntur,
utque pudor cessit sanguisque indūruit ōris,
in rigidum parvō silicem discrīmine versae.
    "Quās quia Pygmaliōn aevum per crīmen agentīs
vīderat, offēnsus vitiīs, quae plūrima mentī
245   fēmineae nātūra dedit, sine coniuge caelebs
vīvēbat thalamīque diū cōnsorte carēbat.
Intereā niveum mīrā fēlīciter arte
sculpsit ebur fōrmamque dedit, quā fēmina nāscī

Discussion Questions

1.   In 241–42 Ovid wants his readers to visualize the actual metamorphosis of the Propoetides, but how might the incident and the transformation also be viewed metaphorically?

2.   Comment on the word order, and its effect, in 242.

3.   What is your response to Pygmalion's actions, and his motivations, in 243–46? Is the characterization of woman's nature (244–45) Pygmalion's, the narrator's (i.e., Orpheus'), or Ovid's?

---

       caelebs, caelibis, *unmarried, celibate.*
246   **thalamus, -ī,** m., *inner chamber; bedroom.*
       cōnsors, cōnsortis, m./f., *one who shares with another; a partner, consort, companion.*
       careō, carēre, caruī, caritūrus + abl., *to lack, be without.*
247   **niveum mīrā fēlīciter arte /** . . . **ebur** (248): the ABCBA arrangement—with the epithets first, and the nouns suspensefully delayed—is as "felicitously artful" as the sculpture Ovid describes. The full significance of **mīrā** becomes apparent as the tale unfolds (cf. **mīrātur** 252).
248   **sculpō, sculpere, sculpsī, sculptus,** *to carve, sculpt.*
       sculpsit ebur, fōrmamque dedit: another chiasmus.
       quā: *(beauty) with which,* abl. of description.
       quā fēmina nāscī / nūlla (249): the alliteration and assonance add a delicate sound effect.

249   **operis . . . suī**: objective gen. with **amōrem** (cf. **simulātī corporis ignēs**
       253).
      *****concipiō, concipere, concēpī, conceptus**, *to receive; to conceive, develop; to*
       express or *compose* (in words).
250   **quam**: subject of both **vīvere** and **velle** in the indirect statement after **crēdās**,
       which you would think was alive and wanted to move; the 2nd-pers. verb
       serves to involve the audience.
251   **reverentia, -ae**, f., *reverence; modesty, shyness* (the statue's imagined
       modesty is quite appropriate, since she is, of course, still nude—see 263).
      movērī: the passive, while essentially equivalent to the English intransitive *to*
       move, is especially suited to the description of a statue which has the will,
       but not the power, *to move itself.*
252   **ars . . . suā**: a brilliant, oxymoronic **sententia**, and certainly a prime tenet in
       Ovid's own philosophy of art.
      haurit / . . . ignēs (253): **ignēs** is used here, as often, of the fires of love,
       with **simulātī corporis**, objective gen.—he *draws into his heart a fiery*
       passion for this body he had created.
253   **simulātī**: a deliberate contrast with **vērae** (250).
254   **operī**: dat. with the compound **admovet**.
      temptantēs: the participle modifies **manūs** but introduces the indirect
       question **an . . . ebur** (255), and so should be translated at the end of the
       main clause, *testing (to see) whether it is flesh or ivory.* The halting
       monosyllables at line's end suspensefully anticipate the question.
255   **corpus . . . fatētur**: the anaphora and the breathless series of dactyls and
       one- and two-syllable words are perhaps meant to suggest Pygmalion's
       excitement as his hands move over the statue's body, an effect continued in
       the alliteration and polysyndeton of the next verse.
256   **dat . . . putat**: Ovid accentuates the internal rhyme by carefully setting the
       rhyming syllables under the ictus.
257   **tāctīs . . . membrīs**: dat. with the compound **īnsīdere**; the separation of
       participle from noun, and in fact the entire structure of the line, is
       precisely paralleled in the next verse.
      īnsīdō, īnsīdere, īnsēdī, īnsessus, *to settle upon; to sink into.*
258   **et . . . artūs**: the prose arrangement would be **et metuit nē līvor in artūs**
       pressōs veniat, and again (as with **tāctīs** 257) English would use a relative
       clause rather than a participle—*and he fears that a bruise may appear on*
       the limbs he has pressed.
      līvor, līvōris, m., *a bluish discoloration, a bruise.*
259   **adhibeō, adhibēre, adhibuī, adhibitus**, *to hold out; to make use of, employ;*
       to offer.
      puellīs: dat. with **grāta**.
260   **mūnera**: like the elegiac lover, Pygmalion showers his beloved with gifts.
      *****concha, -ae**, f., *shellfish* (especially the murex, the ancients' principal source
       for purple dye—see on 267 below); *shell, pearl.*
      teres, teretis, *smooth, rounded.*
      lapillus, -ī, m., *a small stone, pebble; a gem.*

nūlla potest, operisque suī concēpit amōrem.
250 Virginis est vērae faciēs, quam vīvere crēdās
et, sī nōn obstet reverentia, velle movērī—
ars adeō latet arte suā. Mīrātur et haurit
pectore Pygmaliōn simulātī corporis ignēs.
    "Saepe manūs operī temptantēs admovet an sit
255 corpus an illud ebur, nec adhūc ebur esse fatētur.
Ōscula dat reddīque putat, loquiturque tenetque,
et crēdit tāctīs digitōs īnsīdere membrīs,
et metuit pressōs veniat nē līvor in artūs.
Et modo blanditiās adhibet, modo grāta puellīs
260 mūnera fert illī: conchās teretēsque lapillōs
et parvās volucrēs et flōrēs mīlle colōrum
līliaquē pictāsque pilās et ab arbore lāpsās

Discussion Questions

1. Comment on the very striking sound effects in 250–51. How are the halting monosyllables in 251 appropriate to the context?

2. Several elements in the narrative at 247–53 purposely recall the opening tale of the Propoetides (cf., for example, **fōrmam** 248 and **fōrma** 240; **reverentia** 251 and **pudor** 241; **simulātī corporis** 253 and **corpora** 240). Explore the several connections between the description of Pygmalion's statue and the character and transformation of the Propoetides. Why does Ovid link the two stories as he does? How is Pygmalion's reaction to the statue in 252–53 ironic in view of his earlier response to the Propoetides?

3. What do the verbs **putat**, **crēdit**, and **metuit** (256–58) tell us about Pygmalion's emotional state?

---

261 **mīlle colōrum**: gen. of description; and note the assonance with **flōrēs**.
262 **līlium, -ī**, n., *lily.*
        līliaquē: lengthening of a short vowel (diastole) is not uncommon in poetry, especially (as here with **-quē**) when the syllable is under the ictus and precedes a caesura.
    pictus, -a, -um, *painted, colored.*

263   **Hēliades, Hēliadum**, f. pl., *the Heliades* (daughters of the sun god Helios, who, as they lamented the death of their brother Phaethon, were transformed into poplar trees that "wept" tears of amber—Ovid tells the story in *Met.* II).

    lacrimās: here, *amber beads.*

264   ***gemma, -ae**, f., *jewel, gem.*

    monīle, monīlis, n., *necklace, ornamental collar; jewelry.*

265   **aure . . . pectore**: prose would include the prepositions **dē** and **in**, respectively.

    baca, -ae, f., *berry, nut; pearl, bead.*

    redimīculum, -ī, n., *a decorative band, garland.*

266   **Nec . . . vidētur**: litotes; Pygmalion not only dressed his statue, it seems, but also undressed her—for bed!

    ***fōrmōsus, -a, -um**, *beautiful, lovely* (a common epithet in elegy).

267   **collocō, -āre, -āvī, -ātus**, *to set up, arrange.*

    hanc: sc. **statuam**.

    ***strātum, -ī**, n., *bedding, coverlet*; (often in pl.) *bed.*

    Sīdōnis, Sīdōnidis, *of Sidon, Sidonian* (the town of Sidon, on the coast of Phoenicia, was famous for its production and export of purple dye from the murex—see on **concha** 260).

268   **appellō, -āre, -āvī, -ātus**, *to speak to; to call* (someone) *by a particular name.*

        appellatque . . . sociam: sc. **hanc** (from 267)—*and he calls her* (or *it!*) *the companion of his bed* (cf. **thalamī . . . cōnsorte** 246). The alliteration of **l/ll** in this passage adds an elegant sound effect to the scene's close (note especially the soundplay in **collō/collocat/colla** 264–68, and cf. 280 and 285).

    socia, -ae, f., *a female associate, partner.*

    acclīnō, -āre, -āvī, -ātus, *to lay down, rest* (on).

        acclīnāta colla / . . . repōnit (269): *he lays its head to rest.*

269   **plūma, -ae**, f., *feather; feather cushion, pillow.*

    ***tamquam**, conj., *just as, as if, as though.*

        tamquam sēnsūra: *just as though it could feel them.*

    repōnō, repōnere, reposuī, repositus, *to put back; to put down, lay down* (in a position of rest).

270   ***festus, -a, -um**, *festive*; with **diēs** (and often pl.), *a holiday, festival.* The festival of Venus, goddess of sensual love, aptly, and suspensefully, interrupts the bedroom scene of 266–69.

    diēs: often f., as here, when reference is to a specific day.

    tōtā . . . Cyprō: sc. **in**, *the most celebrated in all of Cyprus.*

    Cyprus, -ī, f., *the island of Cyprus.*

271   **pandus, -a, -um**, *curving, bowed.*

    inductae: here, with **aurum** as object and **pandīs . . . cornibus** (dat. with compounds), the participle has a reflexive or middle force, lit. *having applied gold to their arching horns*, but more freely, *with their arching horns gilded*; the entire phrase modifies **iuvencae** (272).

Hēliadum lacrimās. Ōrnat quoque vestibus artūs,
dat digitīs gemmās, dat longa monīlia collō;
265   aure levēs bācae, redimīcula pectore pendent—
cūncta decent. Nec nūda minus fōrmōsa vidētur:
collocat hanc strātīs conchā Sīdōnide tīnctīs,
appellatque torī sociam, acclīnātaque colla
mollibus in plūmīs tamquam sēnsūra repōnit.
270   "Festa diēs Veneris tōtā celeberrima Cyprō
vēnerat, et pandīs inductae cornibus aurum
conciderant ictae niveā cervīce iuvencae,
tūraque fūmābant, cum mūnere fūnctus ad ārās
cōnstitit et timidē 'Sī, dī, dare cūncta potestis,

Discussion Questions

1. What is the intended effect of the polysyndeton in 260–63?

2. Comment on the word order, and its effect, in 264–65.

3. How is the progression of Pygmalion's actions in 254–69 like a courtship? How is it different?

4. Comment on the alliteration in 272. Is the effect onomatopoetic? How do the sound effects of 273 differ?

272   *īciō, īcere, īcī, ictus, *to strike* (with a weapon—here a sacrificial knife or ax).
    niveā cervīce: abl. of respect with ictae.
    iuvenca, -ae, f., *a young cow, heifer* (appropriately, a female animal is sacrificed to the female deity).
273   tūs, tūris, n., *frankincense* (often pl. for the incense used in religious rites).
    fūmō, -āre, -āvī, -ātus, *to fume, (emit) smoke*.
274   timidē: with dīxit (276); Pygmalion addresses the goddess with all due reverence.

275   **coniūnx**: with **mea**. The prose arrangement would be '**Sī, dī, cūncta dare
       potestis, coniūnx mea sit, optō, similis eburnae,**' **Pygmaliōn timidē dīxit**
       (**nōn ausus dīcere 'eburnea virgō'**); in his modesty, Pymalion did not
       dare ask that he marry the statue itself but only some maiden with the
       statue's beauty. The disjointedness of Pygmalion's language here is perhaps
       meant to mirror his hesitancy in making the request.
       optō: used here (as often) parenthetically.
       eburneus, -a, -um, *(made of) ivory*.
276   **eburnus, -a, -um**, *(made of) ivory* (sc. **statuae**).
277   **Sēnsit**: Venus is subject of this verb (cf. 293) as of **aderat**.
       festīs: sc. **diēbus**, dat. with the compound **aderat** (cf. 295).
278   **vōta . . . velint**: indirect question with **sēnsit**; in prose **quid** would introduce
       the clause. Despite the indirection of Pygmalion's prayer, Venus
       understands what he truly wants.
       amīcī . . . ōmen: the phrase (*as an omen* . . .) is in apposition with the signs
       described in 279.
279   **flamma**: i.e., from the incense burning on the altar.
       ter, adv., *three times* (here, as often, a mystical number).
    * **accendō, accendere, accendī, accēnsus**, *to kindle, ignite; to make hotter,
       intensify*.
       apex, apicis, m., *the top or point of something*; here, *the tip* (of a flame).
280   **rediit**: **ille** (Pygmalion) is subject; his return home from the festival and his
       rush to find the statue are described entirely in quick dactyls.
       simulācra: the word, an emphatic pl., perhaps deliberately recalls **similis**
       (276); there Pygmalion prays for a wife *like his ivory statue*, while here his
       statue is *the likeness of his very own girl*. **Suae** is likewise emphatic, as is
       petit, a verb connoting intentional action; and, in anticipation of the
       transformation to come, Ovid describes the statue here for the first time
       with the noun **puella**, a word straight out of the vocabulary of Latin elegy
       (cf. Catullus' frequent, and insistent, **mea puella**). The **ll** alliteration (a
       favorite Catullan sound effect) in **ille puellae** adds a further elegiac touch
       (see on 268).
281   **dedit ōscula**: a deliberate echo of **ōscula dat** (256—and cf. **dataque ōscula**
       292), just as **Admovet . . . manibus . . . temptat** in the next verse looks
       back to **manūs . . . temptantēs admovet** (254), and **subsīdit digitīs** (284)
       recalls **digitōs īnsīdere** (257)—the earlier seduction resumes, but now
       under Venus' inspiration.
       vīsa tepēre est: sc. **statua** or **puella**; the ivory maiden grew warm with life
       and with passion. The preceding diaeresis and the very brevity of the
       clause itself (cf. **Corpus erat** 289) focus our attention on this first sign of
       the statue's animation; Pygmalion here plays the handsome prince to his
       Sleeping Beauty, as his kiss brings her to life.
282   **Admovet . . . temptat**: the seduction proceeds again from kiss to caress (cf.
       256–58); chiasmus intensifies the eroticism by bringing **ōs, manibus**, and
       pectora together, with the verbs framing the scene. The root meaning of
       temptāre, *to feel*, is the correct sense here (and with **vēnae** 289, where

275   sit coniūnx, optō' (nōn ausus 'eburnea virgō'
dīcere), Pygmaliōn 'similis mea,' dīxit, 'eburnae.'
Sēnsit, ut ipsa suīs aderat Venus aurea festīs,
vōta quid illa velint, et, amīcī nūminis ōmen,
flamma ter accēnsa est apicemque per āera dūxit.
280   "Ut rediit, simulācra suae petit ille puellae,
incumbēnsque torō dedit ōscula; vīsa tepēre est.
Admovet ōs iterum, manibus quoque pectora temptat;
temptātum mollēscit ebur, positōque rigōre
subsīdit digitīs cēditque, ut Hymettia sōle

Discussion Question

The references to Venus and her **nūmen** in 270–79 again recall the
narrative's opening lines. In what ways do the Propoetides' treatment of
Venus and her response compare with Pygmalion's attitude toward the
goddess and her response to him? Consider again how the fate of the
Propoetides compares with the fate of Pygmalion's statue.

Pygmalion tests his beauty's pulse), but the word's repetition in this context
(at 282, 283, 289, and cf. 254) strongly suggests its common metaphorical
sense of *making a sexual advance* upon a woman.

temptat; / temptātum (283): the immediate (and alliterative) repetition
underscores the rapidity of the transformation.

283   **mollēscō, mollēscere**, *to become soft* or *yielding* (cf. **remollēscit** 285).

positō: = **dēpositō**; use of the simple form of a verb in place of an expected
compound form is common in verse.

rigōre: cf. the Propoetides' transformation to **rigidum . . . silicem** (242).

284   **subsīdō, subsīdere, subsēdī**, *to crouch down*; + dat., *to yield, give way to*
(some outside force).

    subsīdit digitīs: the sense of the verb here is clarified by the following
simile; Pygmalion's fingers leave their imprint on the statue's flesh in
fact, just as he had fantasized they might in 257.

Hymettius, -a, -um, *from Mt. Hymettus* (a mountain near Athens noted for
its honey and so also, as here, for its beeswax).

285   ***cēra, -ae**, f., *beeswax, wax* (in any of its various uses, including, as here, modeling); *a writing tablet* (of the common type which was coated with wax, on which notes could be easily incised and erased).

    remollēscō, remollēscere, *to become soft again* (cf. **mollēscit** 283).

      remollēscit . . . pollice: for the alliteration see on 268.

    tractō, -āre, -āvī, -ātus, *to keep pulling, dragging; to handle, rub, stroke.*

      tractātaque pollice: wax used for modelling or other purposes was left in the sun and then worked with the fingers to make it softer and thus more readily shaped.

    *pollex, pollicis, m., *thumb.*

    multās: with **faciēs** (286), here *shapes* or *forms.*

286   **flectitur . . . ūsū**: sound effects are added by the alliteration of **f** and the aptly soft assonance of **ū** at the end of the verse (where there is also some etymologizing wordplay in **ūtilis ūsū**).

    fit ūtilis ūsū: the more it is used, or rather handled, the more easily worked and usable the wax becomes.

287   **dubiē**, adv., *hesitatingly, with hesitation.*

    fallīque verētur: sc. **sē**, acc. subject of the infin. in indirect statement.

288   **vōta**: here, not *prayers*, but *the object of his prayers.*

    retractō, -āre, -āvī, -ātus, *to draw back; to handle* or *feel again* or *repeatedly* (cf. **tractāta** 285).

289   **Corpus erat**: the brevity of the clause and its placement at the beginning of the verse underscore Pygmalion's astonishment.

    saliō, salīre, saluī, saltus, *to jump, leap; to move suddenly, pulse.*

    *vēna, -ae, f., *blood-vessel, vein; vein, streak* (of some stone or mineral).

290   **Paphius, -a, -um**, *of Paphos* (a city in southwest Cyprus).

    Paphius . . . hērōs: cf. **Rhodopēius . . . hērōs**, of Orpheus (X.50); and note the interlocking word order in **Paphius . . . / verba** (291). The use of the epithet here anticipates the naming of the city after Pygmalion's child, referred to in 297.

    plēnissima: here, *the most abundant* or *generous.*

291   **grātēs, grātium**, f. pl., *thanks, thanksgiving*; with **agere**, *to give thanks.*

    agit: some mss. have **agat**, and editors accepting that reading view the clause as a relative clause of purpose. But, given Pygmalion's piety in 270-79, the indicative seems preferable—in gratitude he offers a prayer of thanks to the goddess at the very moment of his dream's fulfillment.

    ōra . . . falsa (292): the use of pl. for sing. is common with **ōs**, but may be intentionally emphatic here; note too the effect of the framing order, the suspenseful delay of **nōn falsa**, the wordplay with **ōra/ōre/ōscula**, and the repeated **ō**'s in 292 that suggest the lovers' impassioned moaning.

293   **sēnsit**: the same verb is used of both Venus herself (277) and the lover she has brought to life for Pygmalion; both are sensitive and sensual.

    ērubēscō, ērubēscere, ērubuī, *to blush with shame, feel shame.*

      ērubuit: Pygmalion's creation had the sense of shame and modesty which the Propoetides lacked (cf. **pudor cessit** 241).

    timidum: a trait the girl shares with Pygmalion (cf. **timidē** 274)

285   cēra remollēscit tractātaque pollice multās
      flectitur in faciēs ipsōque fit ūtilis ūsū.
      Dum stupet et dubiē gaudet fallīque verētur,
      rūrsus amāns rūrsusque manū sua vōta retractat.
      Corpus erat: saliunt temptātae pollice vēnae!
290   "Tum vērō Paphius plēnissima concipit hērōs
      verba, quibus Venerī grātēs agit, ōraque tandem
      ōre suō nōn falsa premit, dataque ōscula virgō
      sēnsit et ērubuit, timidumque ad lūmina lūmen
      attollēns pariter cum caelō vīdit amantem.

Discussion Questions

1. Discuss the effectiveness and appropriateness of the simile in 284–86. Notice how the words **remollēscit tractātaque pollice** (285) are connected to identical or closely related words in the surrounding narrative; consider the imagery and the implications of these interconnections.

2. In what respects do diction and sound effects lend intensity to the scene described in 288?

3. How does Ovid's manipulation of verb tenses enliven the narrative in 280–89?

4. Comment on the sound effects in 293.

---

lūmina lūmen: the juxtaposition neatly suits the action, as the statue, now alive, raises *her timid gaze up to his*, and the lovers' eyes meet for the very first time.

294   **pariter,** adv., *together; at the same time.*

      pariter . . . vīdit: *at the very same time she saw both her lover and the light of her first day.* With **cum caelō** there is a play on the double sense of **lūmen** as both *eye(s)* and *light*, and the resulting imagery is brilliant—as Pygmalion's creation opens her eyes, she raises them upward like a newborn child into the light of day and then, in the very same instant, like a blushing maiden, she gazes into the eyes of her lover.

295 **coniugium, -ī,** n., *marriage* (here dat. with the compound **adest**—cf. 277).
  quod fēcit: i.e., through her inspiration and her response to Pygmalion's
  prayer.
  coāctīs / . . . orbem (296): *with the horns of the (crescent) moon brought*
  nine times to full circle, an epic circumlocution for the passage of nine
  months, the length of a pregnancy; interlocking word order and the **n/m**
  alliteration add to the solemn tone.
296 **noviēns,** adv., *nine times*.
  lūnāris, -is, -e, *of the moon*.
297 **illa:** Pygmalion's bride, who remains nameless to the very end of the tale
  (though later writers call her Galatea).
  Paphos, -ī, acc. **Paphon,** f. (or m., as some texts read **dē quō** for **dē quā** in
  this line), *Paphos* (child of Pygmalion).
  gignō, gignere, genuī, genitus, *to create, give birth to*.
  dē quā tenet īnsula nōmen: *from whom the island preserves this name*, i.e.,
  for the city of Paphos (see on **Paphius** 290), a final etiological detail.

"Pygmalion and Galatea," Jean-Léon Gérôme, 1890
Metropolitan Museum of Art, New York

295   "Coniugiō, quod fēcit, adest dea, iamque coāctīs
      cornibus in plēnum noviēns lūnāribus orbem
      illa Paphon genuit, dē quā tenet īnsula nōmen."

Discussion Questions

1. On the surface level of this narrative, Pygmalion may seem to be some kind
   of pervert with a bizarre fetish for his female statue, but in the end of course,
   as the statue is miraculously brought to life, we realize that we have been
   drawn out of the real world and into the world of magic and metamorphosis.
   With this in mind, how might you interpret in metaphorical terms
   Pygmalion's withdrawal from society and his surrender to art? Discuss the
   themes of art, its effects, and its relationship to reality as they are developed
   through the symbolism of the entire narrative.

2. Comment on the function of the statue as a character in the story and
   especially on the paradox that, while central to the tale, she remains utterly
   passive. How are Pygmalion and Ovid alike in their relation to the character?
   What other correspondences do you detect between the poet and the sculptor?

"Pygmalion and Galatea"
Étienne-Maurice Falconet, 1763
Musée des Arts Décoratifs
Paris

THE *AMORES*

In the six selections from the *Amores* that close out this volume, we cross over the boundary from the epic world into the elegiac, and yet as noted in the introduction (which readers may wish to review at this point), that boundary is seldom in Ovid very clearly defined; gods and heroes like Apollo and Orpheus are transformed, so to speak, and cross over the *līmen*, while the elegiac lover joins Cupid's army, brandishes his weapons, and wages his own wars of the night. A brief overview of the individual poems may tempt the reader likewise to escape for a moment into Ovid's Fantasyland, where Cupid reigns triumphant, where real wars and violence are bid farewell, and where Good Sense is held prisoner by Love.

The prefatory I.1 announces the poet's intention to write romantic verse—not, alas, his original plan, but savage Cupid had chuckled, sneaked out a foot from his epic's every second verse, and turned his song from weaponry to love. Transfixed by one of those surefire arrows that would later (in the *Metamorphoses*) inflame Apollo's passion for Daphne, Ovid bids farewell to "iron war" and invokes a Muse he will measure out in the eleven unheroically limping feet of elegy's couplets.

The sequel in I.2, like some 1950s rock-and-roll tune, opens dramatically with poor Ovid, blankets thrown to the floor, "tossing and turning all night." Clearly Love's arrows have taken effect, and the time to surrender is at hand. The poet invites Cupid to celebrate his conquest in triumphal procession, just like a victorious Roman general, except that his chariot will be golden and drawn by doves, his lieutenants will be "Sweet-talk, Miscalculation, and Madness," and his prisoners-of-war will include not only all the world's young lovers but also, bound in chains, "Good Sense and Chastity." In the poem's closing lines, Cupid is first likened to Bacchus (a kindred spirit who similarly exults in passion) and then implored to follow the example of his "kinsman Caesar" and bestow mercy on those he has conquered, the poet among them—a curious allusion to an emperor who in the end would show Ovid himself very little of the much vaunted Caesarian *clementia*.

Poem I.9 is a clever tour de force arguing the thesis that "every lover is truly a soldier, and Commander Cupid has his own camp," an elaboration of the military imagery seen in the previous selections and a variant on a stock rhetorical exercise, which Ovid had doubtless encountered in his own schooling, comparing the soldier's life with the lawyer's. Lovers and soldiers alike must be youthful, vigorous, and brave, prepared for long marches, spy missions, breaking down doors (their mistresses' or their foes'), and launching night attacks. In the tradition of the great heroes at Troy and even of Mars himself—who performed double-duty as both god of war and Venus' lover—Ovid is a true man of action, never the slacker, ever prepared to raise up his sword and wage Cupid's battles in the night. ·

Poems I.11 and 12 both describe a diptych, a Roman writing tablet consisting of two wax-covered boards hinged to fold over at the center, and form one. Page one, I.11, focuses initially on Nape, Ovid's veteran maidservant and go-between, whom he praises for her loyalty, her ingenuity, and her past successes in coaxing Corinna, the poet's mistress, to visit him in the night. Now, brusquely ordering Nape to deliver a love-letter to Corinna, the poet fantasizes that the tablet itself, inscribed with his own charming words, will accomplish the mission; this most faithful of servants will return with just the right message from Corinna— "Come!"—and be garlanded with laurel for the victory. Page two, I.12, a lamentation: Nape had stubbed her toe at the door when setting out (a BAD SIGN!) and the (now fully personified) Diptych itself has come home, sad-faced, with the miserable message, "Can't!" Through the rest of the poem Ovid rewards the unfortunate Tablet and its "notes that say 'No'," not with a garland, but with a gleeful curse on its blood-red wax and its gallows-wood for their ill-omened, loveless "duplicity."

Finally, just as I.1 had been a farewell to arms, as it were, our last selection, *Amores* III.15, bids farewell to Venus and Cupid and to the poet's "warless elegies" (*imbellēs elegī*). But with his own characteristic duplicity, Ovid infuses the poem with a series of military images, announcing in the end that he will steer his war horses next across an even greater field, the *Metamorphoses* and the *Fasti*, he means, which he was soon to commence. In the poem's (and the book's) closing couplet, he expresses his hope that the *Amores* might survive beyond his own death—a well-founded hope, we must surely concede, as we venture forth into the territory of his Cupid poems some two thousand years after their publication.

P. OVIDI NASONIS AMORVM

EPIGRAMMA IPSIVS

Quī modo Nāsōnis fuerāmus quīnque libellī,
   trēs sumus; hoc illī praetulit auctor opus.
Ut iam nūlla tibī nōs sit lēgisse voluptās,
   at levior dēmptīs poena duōbus erit.

Preface to the second edition of the Amores

1   **Arma**: Ovid aptly begins his prefatory, anti-epic elegy with the same
dramatic word (and the same metonymy for *violence* or *war*) that opens
Vergil's *Aeneid*; the somber tone is temporarily continued in **gravī numerō
violentaque bella**, so that by the end of this first verse a listening audience
might suppose that it is about to hear an epic recited. In a later poem (*Am.*
II.1.11–16) Ovid tells us (again doubtless in jest) that the epic he had
started to write was about the battle between the gods and the hundred-
handed giants.

    gravī numerō: here, *in solemn meter*; this reference to dactylic hexameter as
the proper form for epic is, through ring composition, taken up again in
the poem's penultimate couplet (cf. **numerō violentaque bella** and **modīs**,
1–2, with **numerīs** and **ferrea cum vestrīs bella . . . modīs**, 27–28).
Aptly, the rhythm of this opening line, and the first half of the next, is
entirely dactylic.

    violentus, -a, -um, *violent, savage, aggressive*.

2   **ēdō, ēdere, ēdidī. ēditus**, *to give forth, emit; to narrate, publish*.

    ***māteria, -ae**, f., *wood* (as a building material); *material, subject-matter*.

    modīs: here (and in 28, and cf. **ēmodulanda** 30), *rhythms*; dat. with the
compound **conveniente** (cf. line 19).

3   **pār, paris**, *equal* (in measure or magnitude).

        Pār . . . versus: in the dactylic hexameter, of course, every verse has
six feet.

    īnferior, -ius, *lower; following, subsequent* (here referring to the second
verse of a poem or couplet, specifically the elegiac couplet in which this
poem is written).

    rīsisse . . . surripuisse (4): assonance and similar line positioning help link
the two infinitives and underscore the point that Cupid's larceny was to
him a wonderful practical joke.

4   **dīcitur**: by the poet's friends? his audience? his detractors?—the passive is
deliberately ambiguous.

    surripuisse: the verb comically implies a sneaky, surreptitious theft.

    pedem: here (and cf. 30), of course, a metrical *foot*, or rather the two half-
feet which the elegiac's pentameter lacked.

5   **Quis . . . iūris**: for the complaining question, and the provocative epithet
applied to Cupid, cf. *Met.* I.456 above; and for the god's **saevitia**, cf.
saeva Cupīdinis īra (*Met.* I.453). The speaker in 5–20 is the poet himself,
in an earlier moment when he was still contemplating writing epic; **questus
eram** closes out his harangue in 21.

    Quis . . . Quid (7) **. . . Quis** (9) **. . . quis** (11): the series of interrogative
pronouns, the first three placed at the beginning of a couplet, and the
barrage of rhetorical questions in 5–16 underscore the poet's indignation.

    hoc: here (as often with both **hoc** and **hic**), the word is scanned long though
the vowel is short (see on **hic** *Met.* IV.150).

    in carmina: *over poetry* (**in** often has this meaning with **iūs**).

    iūris: partitive gen. with **hoc**, *this authority*.

6   **Pīeris, Pīeridos**, gen. pl. **Pīeridum**, *daughter of Pierus, a Muse* (a common

AMORES I.1

"A Farewell to Arms"

Arma gravī numerō violentaque bella parābam
    ēdere, māteriā conveniente modīs.
Pār erat īnferior versus; rīsisse Cupīdō
    dīcitur atque ūnum surripuisse pedem.
5   "Quis tibi, saeve puer, dedit hoc in carmina iūris?
    Pīeridum vātēs, nōn tua, turba sumus!
Quid, sī praeripiat flāvae Venus arma Minervae,

Discussion Question

Compare the poet's complaint to Cupid in 1–6 with Apollo's complaint in
Met. I.456–62. Who prevailed in the earlier narrative? Who do you suppose
will prevail here? What is the point of these correspondences in the
characterization of Cupid?

---

    patronymic form—Pierus, King of Emathia in Macedonia, was in some
    accounts father of the Muses).
   Pīeridum: with **turba**, the predicate noun.
vātēs: Ovid uses this solemn term for poets as *inspired bards* with mock
   solemnity; here subject of **sumus**, *we bards*.
7   **Quid**: i.e., *What would we think*; the two clauses following constitute the
   protasis to this understood apodosis.
   praeripiō, praeripere, praeripuī, praereptus, *to seize first, snatch away*.
     praeripiat: the verb recalls **surripuisse** (4) and makes a
      distinction—Venus' imagined theft is brazen and violent, while her
      son's is surreptitious.
  ***flāvus, -a, -um**, *yellow; fair-haired, blonde* (a frequent epithet of Minerva).
   arma: the poem's opening word is deliberately recalled; and in the neat
   juxtaposition **Venus arma**, Venus' imagined usurpation of Minerva's
   weapons of war parallels her son Cupid's obstruction of the poet's desire to
   write poems of war rather than love.
  ***Minerva, -ae**, f., *Minerva* (goddess of wisdom and warfare).

8 **ventilō, -āre, -āvī, -ātus**, *to fan* (here, *to fan the flames of*).
accēnsās . . . facēs: i.e., the flames of passion kindled by Venus; note the chiasmus, with **flāva Minerva** at the center, and cf. the deliberately opposite arrangement in 7.

9 **probō, -āre, -āvī, -ātus**, *to approve, commend*; with acc. + infin., *to consider it proper* (for someone to do something).
silvīs . . . iugōsīs: forests were properly the domain of Diana, not of Ceres.
***rēgnō, -āre, -āvī, -ātus**, *to rule, govern, reign*.
iugōsus, -a, -um, *hilly, mountainous*.

10 **lēge**: the word picks up the notion in **rēgnāre** in the preceding verse; within his or her proper sphere, each deity governs by divine law.
pharetrātus, -a, -um, *quiver-bearing* (bow and arrows were Diana's emblem, as they were her brother Apollo's—cf. *Met.* I.456-65).
arva colī: an acc. + infin. phrase after **probet**, paralleling **Cererem rēgnāre** in 9.

11 **Crīnibus**: abl. of respect, with **īnsignem**; Apollo was commonly depicted with long curly locks.
īnsignis, -is, -e, *conspicuous, remarkable* (in appearance).
īnsignem . . . acūtā cuspide Phoebum / . . . Āoniam Marte movente lyram (12): note the reverse chiastic arrangement of these two phrases (adj. A / adj. B / noun-emblem B / noun-deity A, line 11; adj. A / noun-deity B / adj. B / noun-emblem A, line 12), and cf. 7-8; the word order suits the imagined role reversals.

12 **īnstruō, īnstruere, īnstrūxī, īnstrūctus**, *to build*; + abl., *to equip, furnish*.
Āonius, -a, -um, *of Aonia, Boeotian* (Aonia was that region of the Greek district of Boeotia where Mt. Helicon was located—a precinct sacred to the Muses and Apollo).
***Mars, Martis**, m., *Mars* (Roman god of agriculture and especially of war, humorously imagined here strumming Apollo's lyre rather than brandishing a spear, which was his usual attribute).
***lyra, -ae**, f., *a lyre* (a stringed instrument sacred to Apollo and a symbol of lyric poetry).

13 **tibi**: dat. of possession.
magna . . . rēgna: the wide separation of adj. and noun suggests the expansiveness of Cupid's realm; cf. **rēgnat Amor** (26).
puer: cf. line 5; after the three couplets (7-12) each describing role reversals between a pair of gods, the poet again addresses Cupid directly and accusingly.

14 **affectō, -āre, -āvī, -ātus**, *to attempt; to strive for, aspire to*.
ambitiōsus, -a, -um, *self-seeking, ambitious*.

15 **An . . . est**: the full expression would be **An id quod ubīque tuum est**, *Or is all that is everywhere yours*.
ubīque, adv., *anywhere, everywhere*.
Helicōnius, -a, -um, *of Helicon* (a mountain in Boeotia sacred, not to Cupid, but to Apollo and the Muses).
tempē, Greek n. pl. (but sing. in meaning), *valley* (a generalized term taken

ventilet accēnsās flāva Minerva facēs?
Quis probet in silvīs Cererem rēgnāre iugōsīs,
10   lēge pharetrātae virginis arva colī?
Crīnibus īnsignem quis acūtā cuspide Phoebum
    īnstruat, Āoniam Marte movente lyram?
Sunt tibi magna, puer, nimiumque potentia rēgna—
    cur opus affectās, ambitiōse, novum?
15 An quod ubīque tuum est? Tua sunt Helicōnia tempē?
    Vix etiam Phoebō iam lyra tūta sua est?

Discussion Questions

1. How is the word order in 7–8 appropriate to the hypothetical circumstances the poet describes?

2. Discuss in detail the three pairs of examples in 7–12. What is the significance of each pair? How are the visual images incongruous? What are the interconnections among the three pairs? How is the progression from Venus/Minerva to Apollo/Mars especially effective, and what do those two couplets have in common in their conception and imagery? How is the comparison in 11–12 especially suited to the overall subject of the poem?

3. What is the effect of the chiasmus **magna . . . rēgna / . . . opus . . . novum** (13–14)?

4. What is the tone of the short, rapid-fire questions in 15–16?

from Tempe, the valley of the Peneus river in Thessaly—see on **Pēnēius**
Met. I.452 above).
16   **Vix . . . est**: the notion of this line deliberately evokes the image in 11–12.

17 **Cum . . . surrēxit**: a **cum** temporal clause. The verb **surgere**, lit. *to rise to one's feet*, along with **attenuat nervōs** (*weakens my muscles*) in the next line, plays on the metaphor of the metrical *foot* in **pedem** (4)/**pedēs** (30), *When my brand-new page had gotten off on just the right foot with the first verse*. This image of the poet's work coming to life is continued with **surgat** and **resīdat** in 27 and in both passages there seems to be a deliberate sexual double entendre (**nervus**, **opus**, and **surgere** are all commonly used of the male sexual apparatus, as are metaphorical allusions to both the bow and the lyre with their strings which are alternately stretched taut and then relaxed).

   pāgina, -ae, f., *page.*

18 **attenuō, -āre, -āvī, -ātus**, *to make thin; to weaken.*

   nervōs . . . meōs: notice the internal rhyme, with adjective and noun set at the caesura and line's end; the same device appears in 20, 22, and 28.

   proximus, -a, -um, *nearest; next, immediately following.*

   proximus ille: possibly Ovid means Cupid (*then that fellow immediately . . .*), thus repeating the image of the god's theft of a metrical foot in 3–4 (and cf. the assonant **prōtinus ille** 21 and **puer ille** 25, both referring to Cupid). But it is perhaps more likely that the poet is still in 17–18 addressing Cupid directly, as he was in 5–16, and that by **proximus ille** he refers to *the very next (verse)* itself, i.e., the **īnferior versus** of line 3; that pentameter verse, missing a foot, is lame, so to speak, and thus diminishes the poet's strength. A similar personification is certainly intended in 27–28.

19 **mihi**: dat. of possession.

   māteria . . . apta: cf. **māteriā . . . modīs** (2).

   numerīs leviōribus: i.e., the elegiac couplet; dat. with **apta**.

20 **aut puer aut . . . puella**: the poet has neither a boyfriend nor a girlfriend to inspire elegiac verse; the flippant homosexual reference is a convention of the genre.

   longās . . . comās: acc. of respect with **cōmpta**, freely, *with her long tresses beautifully arranged.*

21 **Questus eram . . . cum prōtinus**: sc. **sīc**, *I had complained in just this way, when suddenly . . .* ; the **cum** temporal clause following has **ille** (Cupid) as subject of the three verbs, **lēgit** (22), **lūnāvit** (23), and **dīxit** (24).

   pharetrā . . . solūtā: sc. **ex**.

   solūtus, -a, -um, *unbound, loosened* (here, with **pharetrā**, *opened*).

22 *****legō, legere, lēgī, lēctus**, *to gather, collect, select; to read.*

   exitium, -ī, n., *death, destruction.*

   in exitium . . . meum: acc. of purpose, *for my destruction.*

   spīculum, -ī, n., *a sharp point; a pointed weapon* (here, *an arrow*).

23 **lūnō, -āre, -āvī, -ātus**, *to make crescent-shaped, bend back.*

   genū, -ūs, n., *knee* (here sc. **in**).

   sinuōsus, -a, -um, *bent, curved.*

24 **"Quod"que . . . "opus"**: the prose order would be **dīxitque, "Vātēs, accipe opus quod canās"**; Cupid sarcastically calls Ovid by the elevated

Cum bene surrēxit versū nova pāgina prīmō,
    attenuat nervōs proximus ille meōs.
Nec mihi māteria est numerīs leviōribus apta,
20   aut puer aut longās cōmpta puella comās."
Questus eram, pharetrā cum prōtinus ille solūtā
    lēgit in exitium spīcula facta meum,
lūnāvitque genū sinuōsum fortiter arcum,
    "Quod"que "canās, vātēs, accipe," dīxit, "opus."
25 Mē miserum! Certās habuit puer ille sagittās:
    ūror, et in vacuō pectore rēgnat Amor.

Discussion Questions

1.   In what several respects do 17–20, the last four lines of the poet's complaint to Cupid, recall 1–4, the poem's opening lines?

2.   How is the description of Cupid's actions in 21–26 connected with the imagery of the poem's first verse? What is the purpose of this connection?

3.   Comment on the several correspondences between Apollo's complaint over Cupid's power in *Met*. I.519–20 and the poet's outcry here in 25–26.

---

term he had used of himself in 6, *Oh Holy Bard, here's a genre for you to chant!* So saying, the love god shoots the poor poet with a passion-dart, thus providing him with the inspiration for writing elegy which he had claimed to lack in 19–20. The rel. clause indicates purpose, hence the subjn. mood.

opus: here, and in 27, the word is used of a literary *genre* (and with a possible sexual allusion as well—see on 17).

25   **Mē miserum**: acc. of exclamation.
     Certās . . . sagittās: for the power of Cupid's arrows, cf. *Met*. I.456–73.

26   **ūror . . . Amor**: cf. **pectore tōtō / ūritur** of Cupid's effect on Apollo in *Met*. I.495–96; assonance interconnects the line's key words, **ūror**, **pectore**, and **Amor**.
     vacuō pectore: the reason for the poet's *empty heart* is given in 19–20; and cf. *Met*. I.520.
     rēgnat Amor: Ovid deliberately recalls the images evoked in **Cererem rēgnāre** (9) and **magna . . . rēgna** (13).

27 **surgat . . . resīdat**: not just a prosaic *rise* and *fall*, but *stand up* and *sit down*; Ovid not only continues the imagery of 17–18 (the line with six feet can stand while the lame pentameter cannot) but also has in mind the fact that epic poets would generally rise to recite their verse, whereas more mundane works would often be read sitting down. The subject **opus** and the phrase **in (sex or quīnque) numerīs** should be taken with both verbs.

numerīs . . . / ferrea cum vestrīs bella . . . modīs (28): for the ring composition, evoking the poem's opening lines, see on **gravī numerō** (1). Note also the interlocked order of adjectives and nouns in 28.

resīdō, resīdere, resēdī, *to sit down*.

28 **ferreus, -a, -um**, *made of iron; cruel, violent* (suggesting, by a common synecdoche, the weapons of war).

valēte: the personification of genre, form, and subject is continued with this verb of farewell; cf. the farewell to genre and Muse in Ovid's final elegy, *Am.* III.15.19–20.

29 **Cingere**: pass. imper. with reflexive force (sometimes called the middle voice); with **flāventia tempora**, *bind your golden tresses*.

lītoreus, -a, -um, *of* or *from the seashore*.

lītoreā . . . myrtō: the sea-myrtle (here f. gender) was sacred to Cupid's mother Venus, who was herself born from the sea, and hence a garland of its leaves is appropriately worn by Ovid's lyric Muse; cf. *Am.* I.2.23 below.

flāvēns, flāventis, *golden, yellow*.

tempus, temporis, n., *the side of the forehead, temple* (with **flāventia** here of the hair flowing down the Muse's head).

30 **Mūsa, -ae**, f., *Muse* (one of the nine goddesses of the arts, associated with Apollo—of the nine, Erato in particular was associated with lyric verse and was usually depicted wearing a garland of myrtle).

Ovid's invocation of his Muse, which might otherwise be expected nearer the beginning of the poem, comes aptly here in the closing couplet, since this piece serves as preface to the entire first book of the *Amores*.

per . . . pedēs: as often is the case, English would likelier use a relative clause than the participial phrase, *who will have to be measured out eleven feet at a time!* This final comic reference to the 11 feet of elegy—and its limping Muse—deliberately recalls the poem's second couplet, with **ūndēnōs . . . pedēs** in particular echoing **ūnum . . . pedem** (4).

ūndēnī, -ae, -a, pl. adj., *eleven each, eleven at a time*.

ēmodulor, -ārī, *to measure out, regulate; to put into meter* (as the poem's penultimate word, **ēmodulanda** plays on the root word **modīs** in 2 and 28—the Muse will be both *measured out* and melodiously *set to rhythm*).

The closing line's interlocked word order suits the image and neatly balances the arrangement in 28, the one verse a farewell to epic and its meter, the other a welcome to the Muse and metric of elegy.

Sex mihi surgat opus numerīs, in quīnque resīdat;
　　ferrea cum vestrīs bella, valēte, modīs.
Cingere lītoreā flāventia tempora myrtō,
30　　Mūsa per ūndēnōs ēmodulanda pedēs!

Discussion Questions

1. Comment on the word-picture in verse 29.

2. Discuss in detail the several ways in which lines 25–30 provide an effective conclusion to the poem.

3. An overarching image of the poem is that of reversal (of the poet's intentions, of genres, of the roles played by various gods). How is this imagery reinforced through the poem's ring composition and through the word order of individual lines (how many verses can you find with an ABBA arrangement)?

4. What is the overall purpose of the poem? How is it at once both serious and comedic? Why does Ovid make such a point of his original intention to write epic rather than elegy?

"Sappho and Alcaeus," Sir Lawrence Alma-Tadema, 1881
Walters Art Gallery, Baltimore

1 **Esse . . . quod**: the verb is deliberative subjn.; freely, *What can I say the reason is that . . .* ; the question introduces a series of four complaints in 1–4. The line's halting one- and two-syllable words and the harsh dentals and q/c sounds are meant to suggest the poet's agitated state of mind.
   *dūrus, -a, -um, *hard, firm; harsh.*

2 **pallium, -ī**, n., *a cloak; a bedspread, blanket.*
   nostra: = **mea** (1st pers. pl. for sing.—cf. **cēdimus** 9, **porrigimus** 20).
   sedent: here, *stay in place.*

3 ***somnus, -ī**, m., *sleep* (**somnō** is abl. with **vacuus**, i.e., *sleepless*).
   quam longa: sc. **fuit**, *how long a night it has been!*

4 **lassus, -a, -um**, *tired, weary.*
   lassaque versātī corporis ossa: Ovid likes this sort of chiastic arrangement, with the adjectives first, then the nouns (adj. A—adj. B—noun B—noun A); cf. **iactātās . . . flammās** 11, also 20, 42.
   versātī: not just *turned*, but *which has tossed and turned* (cf. **versat** 8).

5 **puto**: although parenthetical (*I would know it—I think*), the word is important, as it anticipates the quick concession in 7–8; the final -o is shortened (systole), as it often is in poetry when not under the ictus (i.e., in an unaccented position in the verse).
   quō . . . amōre: after **sī, quō** is indefinite, *by some romantic passion.*
   temptārer: here, *if I were being assaulted.*

6 **subeō, subīre, subiī, subitus**, irreg., *to go underneath; to come upon* (someone) *stealthily, sneak up on* (a person—see on **subitum** 9).

7 **Sīc erit**: the consideration in 6 leads to this sudden, dramatic realization, which is punctuated by the strong diaeresis.

8 **possideō, possidēre, possēdī, possessus**, *to have in one's control; to take control of, seize.*
   possessa ferus pectora . . . Amor: the interlocking order with adjectives first, nouns following, is another favorite Ovidian arrangement (see on **lassaque . . . ossa** 4); cf. 28, 30, 39, 46, 51. For **possessa . . . versat** (which deliberately recalls **versātī** 4) English would use two verbs, *takes possession of and assails.* With **ferus . . . Amor**, cf. **saeve puer** (*Am.* I.1.5).
   Amor: the indefinite **amōre** of 5 (in the same suspenseful position in the verse), personified in **callidus . . . nocet** (6), here becomes Love himself, i.e., Cupid, as the speaker recognizes that he has been smitten by the god. For the suddenness of the attack and its realization, cf. **subitum** (9).

9 **Cēdimus**: *do I surrender?* Note the sound- and word-play with **accendimus** and **cēdāmus** (identically positioned in 10).
   subitus, -a, -um, *sudden, unexpected* (a deliberate play on **subit** 6).
   luctandō: *by resisting.*
   accendimus ignem: for the metaphor of love's fiery passion, cf. 43–46 below and *Met.* I.495–96 above.

10 **leve . . . onus**: a famous Ovidian **sententia**, which was already a proverb in Ovid's day.

11 **Vīdī . . . vīdī** (12): anaphora encourages the reader's visualization.

AMORES I.2

"The Triumph of Love"

    Esse quid hoc dīcam, quod tam mihi dūra videntur
        strāta, neque in lectō pallia nostra sedent,
et vacuus somnō noctem (quam longa!) perēgī,
        lassaque versātī corporis ossa dolent?
5   Nam, puto, sentīrem, sī quō temptārer amōre—
        an subit et tēctā callidus arte nocet?
    Sīc erit: haesērunt tenuēs in corde sagittae,
        et possessa ferus pectora versat Amor!
    Cēdimus, an subitum luctandō accendimus ignem?
10   Cēdāmus: leve fit, quod bene fertur, onus.
    Vīdī ego iactātās mōtā face crēscere flammās,
        et vīdī nūllō concutiente morī;

Discussion Questions

1.   Comment on the dramatic and visual elements in the poem's opening lines (1–4); what is the mental state of the speaker? How does this opening scene set the stage for what follows?

2.   In what ways do the next two couplets (5–8) connect this poem with the preceding one?

3.   Why does Ovid describe Cupid's arrows as **tenuēs** (7)?

4.   In view of the reference to **sagittae** in 7 and the military imagery that dominates the rest of the poem, what do you regard as the best interpretation of **possessa** and **ferus** in 8? How does word order enhance Ovid's point here?

---

      iactātās mōtā face: freely, *fanned by the movement of a torch*; for the word order, see on 4.
      flammās: subject of both **crēscere** and **morī** (12).
12   **concutiō, concutere, concussī, concussus**, *to shake, agitate.*

13   **verber, verberis**, n., usually pl., *a whip; a beating; a lash, blow* (from a whip or a stick).

    ferunt: the subject is **bovēs**; the prose arrangement would be **Bovēs prēnsī, dum iuga prīma dētractant, plūra verbera ferunt, quam (bovēs) quōs ūsus arātrī iuvat.**

    quōs . . . arātrī: freely, *who delight in the work of the plow* (lit., *whom use of the plow delights*).

    iuvō, iuvāre, iūvī, iūtus, *to help; to delight, give pleasure to.*

    arātrum, -ī, n., *a plow.*

14   **dētractō, -āre, -āvī, -ātus**, *to refuse to undertake, recoil from.*

    prēnsī: here, *when they have been rounded up.*

    iugum, -ī, n., *a yoke* (by which a plow is drawn).

15   **contundō, contundere, contudī, contūsus**, *to pound; to bruise, make sore.*

    ōra: acc. of respect with **contunditur**; cf. *Met.* I.484 above.

    lupāta, -ōrum, n. pl., *a toothed bit* (used with horses difficult to manage).

16   **frēnum, -ī**, n., *bridle, rein.*

    ad arma facit: *adapts to the harness* (lit., *acts with regard to its gear*).

18   **quī**: sc. **eōs** as antecedent and object of **urget**.

    servitium, -ī, n., *slavery, service.*

    Amor: subject of **urget**, suspensefully delayed; the two instances of the word, here and at the end of 8 (each at the end of its sentence and its verse), neatly frame the argument in 9–18, which now, in the speaker's view, has been resolved.

19   **ēn**, interj., *behold, look!*

    cōnfiteor, cōnfitērī, cōnfessus sum, *to admit, confess* (the word deliberately looks back to **fatentur** 18).

    praeda: cf. 29; the word clarifies **servitium**—the speaker is not just Love's slave, he is his prisoner of war!

    Cupīdō: from this point to the end of the poem, the speaker addresses Cupid directly.

20   **porrigō, porrigere, porrēxī, porrēctus**, *to stretch forth, extend.*

    ad tua iūra: i.e., I surrender myself *to your control.*

21   **Nīl**: = **Nōn.**

    bellō: abl. with **opus est.**

22   *****laus, laudis**, f., *praise, glory* (here predicate nom., *nor shall I, an unarmed man, be a source of praise for you, if I am vanquished by your arms*).

    victus: the image of the poet as victim of Love's assault (cf. **victās** 20) is taken up again in the poem's closing lines (cf. **victor** 50 and **vīcit, victōs** 52).

    *****inermis, -is, -e**, *unarmed, defenseless* (for the wordplay with **armīs**, cf. *Am.* I.9.22 below).

23   **nectō, nectere, nexī, nexus**, *to weave; to bind, tie.*

        Necte . . . columbās: with its repeated **n/m** sounds, the line is highly alliterative and is perhaps meant to suggest the hushed cooing of the doves.

    myrtō: see on *Am.* I.1.29 above.

verbera plūra ferunt quam quōs iuvat ūsus arātrī,
    dētractant prēnsī dum iuga prīma, bovēs;
15   asper equus dūrīs contunditur ōra lupātīs:
    frēna minus sentit, quisquis ad arma facit.
Ācrius invītōs multōque ferōcius urget,
    quam quī servitium ferre fatentur, Amor.
Ēn ego, cōnfiteor, tua sum nova praeda, Cupīdō;
20   porrigimus victās ad tua iūra manūs.
Nīl opus est bellō—veniam pācemque rogāmus—
    nec tibi laus, armīs victus inermis, erō.
Necte comam myrtō, māternās iunge columbās;

Discussion Questions

1.   What is the "rhetorical" purpose of the three couplets in 11–16? Comment on the relation of these lines to the point made in 17–18.

2.   How do verses 21–22 in particular evoke the opening of *Am.* I.1?

---

māternus, -a, -um, *of a mother, maternal.*
    iunge columbās / . . . **currum** . . . **dabit** (24) / . . . **datō currū** (25)
    . . . **adiūnctās** . . . **avēs** (26): the extended chiasmus, and the
    correspondence between the verbs and the perfect participles which
    imply their realization, suggest the swiftness of the action as the poet
    imagines it.
   iunge: *yoke* (i.e., to the triumphal chariot described in the following lines).
   columbās: like the myrtle, doves were sacred to Venus, Cupid's mother—but
   these are very special doves indeed, capable of drawing their young
   master's chariot (like the sparrows who drew Aphrodite's chariot in a
   poem by the Greek lyric poetess Sappho).

24 quī deceat: sc. tē; a rel. clause of purpose, describing **currum**.
  *currus, -ūs**, m., *a chariot*.
  vītricus, -ī, m., *a stepfather*.
      vītricus ipse: probably Vulcan is meant, Venus' husband, god of the
      forge; though she had cuckolded him in a relationship with Mars (cf.
      Am. I.9.39–40 below), Venus could charm him into crafting weapons
      for her son Aeneas (as she did in *Aeneid* VIII) or, here, a chariot for
      her other son Cupid (whose real father, according to some accounts,
      was Jupiter).
25 **triumphum**: for the triumphal procession of a victorious general, see on
      Met. I.560.
26 **adiungō, adiungere, adiūnxī, adiūnctus**, *to connect; to yoke, harness*.
  arte movēbis: *you will skilfully direct*.
27 **Dūcentur . . . puellae**: the slow initial spondees and the ordered anaphora
      suit the description of this majestic procession of youths and maidens who
      have become (both literally and figuratively) Love's captives.
28 **haec . . . triumphus**: for the interlocked order, see on 8.
29 **Ipse . . . recēns**: the poet imagines himself as one of the **iuvenēs captī** in the
      god's procession.
  factum modo: *freshly inflicted*; note the chiasmus in **praeda recēns, factum
  modo vulnus**.
30 *vinculum, -ī**, n., *chain, shackle* (usually pl.).
31 **Mēns Bona . . . / et Pudor** (32): personifying the virtues of *Good Sense and
      Chastity*, Ovid imagines them as deities (there were shrines to both in
      Rome) taken prisoner, like himself, by Love and his wild
      companions—*Sweet-talk, Miscalculation, and Madness* (35)—and paraded
      through the streets of Rome in the god's triumphal procession. In part this
      is a humorous reversal of the scene in *Aeneid* I.292–96, where Jupiter
      prophecies the victory of Fidelity (**Fidēs**) over Madness (**Furor**), who is
      similarly depicted with hands bound **post tergum**.
  retorqueō, retorquēre, retorsī, retortus, *to twist around, pull backward*.
32 *castra, -ōrum**, n. pl., *a military camp* (the military imagery continues—and
      cf. the reference to Love's *camp* in *Am.* I.9.1 and 44 below).
  obsum, obesse, obfuī + dat., irreg., *to be a hindrance (to), be a nuisance
  (to)*.
33 **tē . . . tē**: frequent use of the second-person pronoun punctuates the
      speaker's lengthy address to Cupid, which continues to the end of the poem
      (see on 19). Here placement of the word under the ictus heightens the
      effect of the anaphora.
34 *vulgus, -ī**, n., *the common people, the multitude*.
  iō, interj., *oh!* (a ritual shout with **triumphe**—see on *Met.* I.560 above).
35 **error, errōris**, m., *wandering; error, mistake* (here personified).
36 **assiduē**, adv., *continually, constantly*.
      assiduē . . . tuās: the entire participial phrase is in apposition to the
          subjects of the preceding verse; English would use a relative clause, *a
          mob that has constantly trouped along with your party*. The series of

qui deceat, currum vitricus ipse dabit;
25   inque dato curru, populo clamante triumphum,
      stabis et adiunctas arte movebis aves.
   Ducentur capti iuvenes captaeque puellae;
      haec tibi magnificus pompa triumphus erit.
   Ipse ego, praeda recens, factum modo vulnus habebo
30   et nova captiva vincula mente feram.
   Mens Bona ducetur manibus post terga retortis
      et Pudor et castris quidquid Amoris obest.
   Omnia te metuent; ad te sua bracchia tendens,
      vulgus "Io" magna voce "triumphe" canet.
35   Blanditiae comites tibi erunt Errorque Furorque,
      assidue partes turba secuta tuas.
   His tu militibus superas hominesque deosque;
      haec tibi si demas commoda, nudus eris.

Discussion Questions

1. In what respect is the interlocked order of 30 particularly apt?

2. How are the sound effects and the word order in 35 especially effective?

        sibilants and dentals suggests the tittering of this *Passion Brigade* (Peter Green's irresistible translation!).
  partes: here with the sense of *partisans* or even a rollicking, quasi-political "Cupid for President" *party*; all these folks are Love's groupies.
37   **His . . . militibus**: abl. of accompaniment.
  hominesque deosque: the polysyndeton (cf. **Errorque Furorque** 35) adds epic effect; Cupid is master of both heaven and earth!
38   **haec tibi**: a deliberate echo of **His tu** in the preceding verse, to underscore the contrasting ideas; the pronoun is dat. of reference with both **demas** and **commoda**, *if someone should take from you these allies (who are) so advantageous to you.*
  si demas . . . eris: a mixed future condition, tentative in the protasis (hence the generalizing 2nd pers. verb), more vivid in the apodosis.
  nudus: figuratively, *defenseless*, but also with a play on Cupid's usual attire—his birthday suit!

39   **Laeta . . . Olympō**: for the interlocked order, see on verse 8 above; we are reminded for the second time of Venus (cf. **māternās . . . columbās** 23), who rejoices here, like any good mother, in her son's triumph.

    triumphō, -āre, -āvī, -ātūrus, *to celebrate a triumph* (with the participle here sc. **tibi**, dat. with **plaudet**).

40   **plaudō, plaudere, plausī, plausus**, *to clap, applaud* (for).

    appositus, -a, -um, *nearby, at one's side.*

41   **pinna, -ae**, f., *feather, wing* (Cupid was regularly depicted with wings).

        pinnās . . . capillōs: both nouns are objects of the abl. absolute **gemmā variante**; instead of the pl., which might be expected, **gemmā** is repeated to intensify the image.

    variō, -āre, -āvī, -ātus, *to adorn with various colors.*

42   **in aurātīs . . . rotīs**: synecdoche (not just *on golden wheels*, but *in your golden chariot*—cf. *Am.* I.12.14).

43   **Tunc quoque . . . / tunc quoque** (44): i.e., even as he advances in his triumphal chariot; anaphora underscores the point.

    nōn paucōs: i.e., *many* (cf. **multa** 44); litotes.

    nōscō, nōscere, nōvī, nōtus, *to find out, learn*; in perf. tense, *to know* (here again pl. for sing.—see on **nostra** 2).

    ūrēs: the vivid metaphor in 43–46 of lovers wounded by Cupid's assault with fire and arrows purposely recalls the poem's earlier imagery (especially in 7–9 and 29).

45   **licet ipse velīs**: a concessive subjn. clause, *even though you yourself should wish it*; even Cupid cannot control the forces he has unleashed.

46   **fervidus, -a, -um**, *intensely hot, blazing.*

        fervida . . . nocet: the arrows themselves are aflame and their searing heat burns not only those who are struck but any who are too close to their path. The repetition of **v** is perhaps meant to suggest onomatopoetically the whooshing of the arrows through the air (cf. on *Met.* I.528 above); Vergil uses the same alliteration for the sound of rushing winds when he describes Aeneas' vain attempt at embracing Creusa's ghost in *Aen.* II.794, **pār levibus ventīs volucrīque simillima somnō**, an effect brilliantly replicated in C. Day Lewis' translation, *it was like grasping a wisp of wind or the wings of a fleeting dream.*

    vīcīnō . . . vapōre: *when its heat comes too close.*

47   **domō, domāre, domuī, domitus**, *to subdue, tame; to conquer.*

        domitā . . . Gangētide terrā: abl. absolute.

    Bacchus, -ī, m., *Bacchus* (god of vegetation, and especially of wine and its effects on men).

    Gangētis, Gangētidis, f. adj., *of the Ganges* (a river of India, the eastern boundary of Alexander's conquests and Bacchus'—after establishing his cult there, the god returned to Greece in a chariot drawn by leopards).

48   **tū . . . ālitibus, tigribus ille**: chiasmus; take **gravis** (here, *powerful* or *majestic*) also with the second clause and supply **es** with the first.

Laeta triumphantī dē summō māter Olympō
40   plaudet et appositās sparget in ōra rosās.
Tū—pinnās gemmā, gemmā variante capillōs—
     ībis in aurātīs aureus ipse rotīs.
Tunc quoque nōn paucōs (sī tē bene nōvimus) ūrēs;
     tunc quoque praeteriēns vulnera multa dabis.
45   Nōn possunt, licet ipse velīs, cessāre sagittae;
     fervida vīcīnō flamma vapōre nocet.
Tālis erat domitā Bacchus Gangētide terrā—
     tū gravis ālitibus, tigribus ille fuit.
Ergō, cum possim sacrī pars esse triumphī,
50   parce tuās in mē perdere, victor, opēs.

Discussion Questions

1. What are the most striking elements of diction, word order, and sound effect in 41–42? Why is the elaborate structure of this couplet so appropriate to its context?

2. Compare the imagery of 43–44 with that of *Met.* I.493–96 above. How are the two passages alike, and in what significant respects do they differ?

3. Consider Ovid's purposes for the seemingly abrupt comparison of Cupid with Bacchus in 47–48, the final couplet in the description of the god's triumph. In what ways were the two deities alike? How were they different? Ovid's audience knew the story of Bacchus' exploits in India and of his procession in a chariot drawn by leopards; how does Ovid emphasize Cupid's contrasting image in 48, and what is the effect of the contrast?

4. Comment on the sound effects in verse 48.

49   *ergō, conj., *therefore* (a transition word, here, along with the series of spondees, emphatically initiating the poet's epilogue).
     sacrī: a key word, reminding us that Cupid is really a god, not a general, and that his "prisoners" are in fact his devotees; it is in this capacity that Ovid closes with what seems a political entreaty but is instead a prayer.
50   parce: with the infin. perdere, this verb is essentially equivalent to nōlī, *do not waste.*

51   ***aspiciō, aspicere, aspexī, aspectus**, *to look at; to consider, think about.*
     cognātus, -ī, m., *kinsman.*

> **cognātī . . . Caesaris:** the Iulii traced their lineage through the legendary Iulus and his father Aeneas to Venus, mother of both Aeneas (by Anchises) and of Cupid (see, e.g., *Aen.* I.256–88).

     Caesar, Caesaris, m., *Caesar* (a cognomen of the **gēns Iulia** and of the emperors, here Caesar Augustus).

52   **quā: manū** is antecedent.

> **quā vīcit, victōs:** spondees and the deliberate juxtaposition underscore Ovid's point.

     prōtegō, prōtegere, prōtēxī, prōtēctus, *to cover; to protect.*
     ille: identical positioning of the demonstrative here and in 48 leaves the reader wondering about the nuance of a link between Augustus and Bacchus, both of whom are compared with Cupid in the poem's conclusion.

Prima Porta Augustus, with Cupid
Late 1st century B.C.
Vatican Museums, Vatican State

Aspice cognātī fēlīcia Caesaris arma:
   qua vīcit, victōs prōtegit ille manū.

Discussion Questions

1. Within the context of the poet's entire address to Cupid, what do you see as the rhetorical function of the two closing couplets?

2. Comment on the image of victor and vanquished as developed in these concluding lines (49–52). How does the image compare with that in 19–22? What is the relation of verses 23–48 to these framing couplets?

3. What is Ovid's purpose in introducing the reference to Augustus into his final couplet? What is its effect on the mood established throughout the rest of the poem? How do these lines compare, in intent and effect, with the Augustan references in *Met.* I.560–65?

4. Explore the possibility of an intentional link between Bacchus and Augustus in the ways they are associated with Cupid. What might Ovid's point be? In what ways are the two figures analogous? How might Augustus himself have responded to the connection with Cupid or Bacchus?

In the hexameter rises the fountain's silvery column;
   In the pentameter aye falling in melody back.

Samuel Taylor Coleridge (translated from Schiller)
"The Ovidian Elegiac Metre Described and Exemplified"

1   **mīlitō, -āre, -āvī, -ātus,** *to serve as a soldier, perform military service.*

       Mīlitat omnis amāns . . . mīlitat omnis amāns: repetition of this entire clause at the beginning and end of the opening couplet emphatically announces the metaphor (a variant of the love/war metaphor in *Am.* I.2) which the rest of the poem elaborates.

       amāns: here, as elsewhere, = **amātor** (cf. *Met.* I.474).

       castra: cf. *Am.* I.2.32 above.

2 · **Atticus, -ī, m.,** *Atticus* (the poem's addressee, named in a few of Ovid's other poems but not certainly identifiable).

3   **quae:** the rel. pron. and its antecedent **aetās** frame the line in a type of chiasmus.

       habilis, -is, -e + dat., *useful (to), suited (for).*

       Venerī: the goddess represents love in general, of course, just as **bellō** suggests Mars, the god of war; cf. 29 below.

       convenit: here essentially = **est habilis.**

       aetās, aetātis, f., *age, time of life* (here, youth).

4   ***turpis, -is, -e,** *offensive, foul, disgusting; shameful, disgraceful.*

       turpe . . . amor: sc. **est;** the n. adj., *a loathsome thing,* reduces the aged soldier and the aged lover to objects.

       senīlis, -is, -e, *of an old man, in old age, aged.*

          senīlis amor: a neat (and metrically convenient) variation for **senex amāns.**

5   **Quōs petiēre . . . / hōs petit** (6): rhyme and anaphora underscore the parallel Ovid is drawing.

       petiēre: for the form, see on *Met.* I.478.

       animōs: take with both **quōs** and **hōs** (6).

       fortī: prolepsis; i.e., once the soldier has **animōs,** then he will be **fortis.**

6   ***socius, -a, -um,** *keeping company* (with another), (in the role of) *companion; allied.*

       bellus, -a, -um, *beautiful, lovely, charming.*

          bella puella: a favorite phrase in the poetry of Catullus; in this context the adj. is likely a pun on **bellum,** *war* (cf. on **bella** 45).

7   **pervigilō, -āre, -āvī, -ātūrus,** *to stay awake all night.*

       terrā: sc. **in.**

8   **forēs . . . servat:** with both **ille . . . dominae** and **ille ducis;** the lover/soldier *guards the entranceway,* i.e., by sleeping on the ground outside the girlfriend's house or the commander's tent.

9   **via:** here, *march.*

       mitte: = **ēmitte** (on the use of simple for compound verbs, see on *Met.* X.283), *send the girl forth,* i.e., on some mission; the imper. is often used in place of the indic. in the protasis of conditional sentences.

10   **strēnuus . . . amāns:** the adj./noun phrase is aptly extended from the beginning of the verse to the end—another neat Ovidian word-picture, suggesting the *long march* (**longa . . . via** 9) that the *hardy lover* is willing to endure.

       eximō, eximere, exēmī, exēmptus, *to take out, remove.*

AMORES I.9

"Make Love, Not War!"

    Mīlitat omnis amāns, et habet sua castra Cupīdō;
        Attice, crēde mihī, mīlitat omnis amāns!
    Quae bellō est habilis, Venerī quoque convenit aetās:
        turpe senex mīles, turpe senīlis amor.
5   Quōs petiēre ducēs animōs in mīlite fortī,
        hōs petit in sociō bella puella virō.
    Pervigilant ambō, terrā requiēscit uterque;
        ille forēs dominae servat, at ille ducis.
    Mīlitis officium longa est via: mitte puellam,
10   strēnuus exēmptō fīne sequētur amāns.
    Ībit in adversōs montēs duplicātaque nimbō

Discussion Questions

1.   In what ways does the poem's opening couplet (1–2) resume the imagery of *Am.* I.2?

2.   Comment on the anaphora and the word order in 4. What are the intended effects?

3.   Some manuscripts have **annōs** for **animōs** in 5. In view of the context both immediately preceding and following, why is **animōs** more likely what Ovid wrote?

4.   How are the word order and sound effects in 6 especially appropriate to the image?

5.   Compare the arrangement of the love/war images in each of the antithetical pairings in 1–3 and 5–6.

---

      exēmptō fīne: = **sine fīne**, i.e., to the ends of the earth.
11   **ībit in**: lit., *he will go up against*, though one might consider the expression a kind of zeugma, i.e., *he will climb* (**montēs**) and *he will ford* (**flūmina**).
      duplicātus, -a, -um, *doubled in size* (here = *swollen*).
      nimbus, -ī, m., *rain-cloud; rain.*

12 **congestus, -a, -um**, *piled up, accumulated.*
exterō, exterere, exterīvī, exterītus, *to rub away, wear down; to crush.*
***nix, nivis**, f., *snow.*

13 **fretum, -ī**, n., *strait, channel*; sing. or pl., *the sea.*
freta pressūrus: i.e., as he is about to set sail.
tumidōs: here, *violent.*
causor, causārī, causātus sum, *to plead a case; to plead* (about something)
as an excuse (here, as an excuse not to sail).
eurus, -ī, m., *the east wind.*

14 **aptaque verrendīs sīdera . . . aquīs**: *stars suited for sweeping over the seas,*
i.e., skies propitious for sailing; the interlocked order and the sound
effects—both the roaring r's and the assonant -īs/sī-/-īs—help us see and
hear the ship's oars dipping into and out of the sea.
verrō, verrere, versūrus, *to remove dust, sweep; to sweep over, skim the*
surface of.

15 **frīgus, frīgoris**, n., *cold, chill*; often pl., *cold spells, frosts.*

16 **dēnsō . . . nivēs**: a golden line (see on *Met.* I.484 above and cf. 23 below).
perferet: for the intensifying prefix cf. **pervigilant** (7).

17 **Mittitur**: the verb is often used of military missions; cf. **mitte** (9).
Mittitur . . . tenet (18): the entire couplet is an elaborate ABCDEEDCBA
chiasmus, with the corresponding elements **Mittitur/tenet, īnfestōs/ut**
hoste, alter/alter, speculātor/oculōs, in hostēs/in rīvāle.
īnfestus, -a, -um, *hostile; savage, violent.*
īnfestōs . . . hostēs: within the extended chiasmus Ovid uses another
favorite chiastic arrangement, with adjs. first, nouns following, in
acc./nom./nom./acc. order; the *savage foe* "surrounds" the *observer*
(and note the somewhat comparable word-picture in the following
verse).
speculātor, speculātōris, m., *observer, scout, spy.*

18 **in . . . tenet**: the prose order would be **alter oculōs in rīvāle, ut hoste,**
tenet.
rīvālis, rīvālis, m., *a rival* (especially in love—the word means, lit., *one who*
shares with another the use of a stream, **rīvus**, a fascinating etymology!).
oculōs . . . tenet: English has the same idiom, he *keeps his eyes on* . . . .

19 **Ille . . . hic . . . hic . . . ille** (20): chiasmus; the roles assigned to the
different demonstratives are reversed.
gravēs: with **urbēs**, *mighty.*
līmen: this and other words for doors or pathways often have a sexual double
entendre in Latin erotic verse; Ovid may intend such a nuance in this
couplet. Cf. on **arma** (26).
ille forēs: cf. **ille forēs** (8); there the lover was guarding his mistress' door,
here he is breaking it down.

21 **sopōrātus, -a, -um**, *lulled to sleep, asleep.*
invādō, invādere, invāsī, invāsus, *to assault, attack.*

22 **caedō, caedere, cecīdī, caesus**, *to strike; to attack, slaughter.*
caedere et: = et caedere; anastrophe.

flūmina; congestās exteret ille nivēs;
nec, freta pressūrus, tumidōs causābitur eurōs
    aptaque verrendīs sīdera quaeret aquīs.
15 Quis, nisi vel mīles vel amāns, et frīgora noctis
    et dēnsō mixtās perferet imbre nivēs?
Mittitur īnfestōs alter speculātor in hostēs;
    in rīvāle oculōs alter, ut hoste, tenet.
Ille gravēs urbēs, hic dūrae līmen amīcae
20   obsidet; hic portās frangit, at ille forēs.
Saepe sopōrātōs invādere prōfuit hostēs
    caedere et armātā vulgus inerme manū:
sīc fera Thrēiciī cecidērunt agmina Rhēsī,

Discussion Questions

1. How do each of the specific circumstances described in 7–16 support the assertion of 5–6?

2. How are the meter and word order in 16 suited to the action?

3. What is the point of the chiasmus in 17–18?

4. Comment on the word order and the anaphora in 19–20.

---

    armātā vulgus inerme manū: note the assonance, the etymologizing wordplay in **armātā/inerme** (cf. *Am.* I.2.22), and the arrangement which has the *unarmed throng* positioned within the grip, so to speak, of the *armed hand* (cf. 26 below) or (with a different sense of **manus**) surrounded by an *armed band*.

23   **fera . . . Rhēsī**: another golden line (cf. 16 above).

    Thrēicius, -a, -um, *Thracian, of Thrace* (a region of Greece east of Macedon).

    agmen, agminis, n., *stream*; sing. or pl., *army*.

    Rhēsus, -ī, m., *Rhesus* (a Thracian ally of Priam, killed by Ulysses and Diomedes in a night raid).

24   **captī . . . equī**: voc. case. An important purpose of the mission against
       Rhesus was to steal his horses; the apostrophe to those horses here adds a
       touch of mock pathos. The adj./noun placement, producing internal rhyme
       at the pentameter's caesura and line's end, is a favorite Ovidian device, as
       we have seen before (cf. 6 and 14 above, 38, 42, and 44 below).
    dēserō, dēserere, dēseruī, dēsertus, *to leave, desert.*

25   **nempe**, *of course, to be sure.*
    ūtor, ūtī, ūsus sum + abl., *to use, take advantage of.*

26   **sua . . . arma movent**: *they brandish their own weapons*; here, as often in
       Latin, **arma** is intended as a metaphor for the lover's sexual apparatus, a
       point emphasized by **sua** (cf. the similar use of the word in **sua castra** 1
       and **castrīs . . . suīs** 44). For the double entendre, see on **līmen** (19); and
       for the word order, cf. 22.
    sōpītus, -a, -um, *overcome by sleep, sleeping.*
       sōpītīs hostibus: abl. absolute.

27   **vigil, vigilis**, m., *guard, sentry.*

28   **mīlitis . . . opus**: sc. **est**, *it is the task of the soldier* (+ infin.).
    miserī: read with **mīlitis** as well as **amantis**.

29   **Mars dubius, nec certa Venus**: chiasmus; for Mars and Venus, cf. 3 above
       and 39–40 below.
    nec certa: litotes for **dubia**.
    victīque . . . / quōsque (30): correlative conjunctions (*both . . . and*)
       connect the two clauses; the verbs are each set at the end of the verse for
       end-rhyme and to underscore the contrasting images (which again carry a
       sexual double entendre).
    resurgō, resurgere, resurrēxī, resurrēctūrus, *to rise again.*

30   **quōsque**: acc. subject of the indirect statement; sc. **illī**, *and those who you*
       would say could never lie in defeat.
    negēs: potential subjn.

31   **Ergō**: a strong transition word, introducing a central argument of the poem.
    dēsidia, -ae, f., *laziness, idleness; leisure.*
       dēsidiam . . . amōrem: **vocābat** takes a double acc., *whoever was*
          calling love a vacation; placement of the nouns at opposite ends of the
          clause emphasizes the polarity, and the **dēsidiam/dēsinat** (32)
          soundplay underscores the prohibition.
    vocābat: the indic. mood implies some actual character (the Atticus of line 2,
       perhaps), who has been accusing the poet, or the lover in general, of idling
       away his life.

32   **dēsinō, dēsinere, dēsīvī, dēsitus**, *to cease, desist; to stop talking.*
    ingeniī . . . experientis: gen. of description, in place of a predicate nom., *of*
       an enterprising nature (we might say instead, *Love has an enterprising*
       nature).
    experiēns, experientis, *enterprising, active.*
    Amor: because of the characterization here and the references to Mars and
       Venus in 29, we are probably meant to think of Cupid (cf. **Cupīdō** 1) and
       not just **amor** in general.

      et dominum captī dēseruistis equī;
25   nempe marītōrum somnīs ūtuntur amantēs
      et sua sōpītīs hostibus arma movent.
      Custōdum trānsīre manūs vigilumque catervās
      mīlitis et miserī semper amantis opus.
      Mars dubius, nec certa Venus: victīque resurgunt,
30   quōsque negēs umquam posse iacēre, cadunt.
      Ergō, dēsidiam quīcumque vocābat amōrem,
      dēsinat—ingeniī est experientis Amor!
      Ardet in abductā Brīsēide maestus Achillēs
      (dum licet, Argēas frangite, Trōes, opēs);

Discussion Question

What four actions are described in 17–30 and how does this section of the poem differ from 7–16?

---

33   **Ardet . . . Achillēs**: in a story best known from *Iliad* I, Achilles ultimately withdrew from fighting the Trojans because of Agamemnon's seizure of his slave-girl Briseis; in this display of **dēsidia** (31) he is, some readers object, an inappropriate example for Ovid here. But Achilles' first impulse, in a fit of anger, was to slay the king—hence **ardet**, which implies his hostility toward the Greek chieftain as much as his passion for Briseis.
    abdūcō, abdūcere, abduxī, abductus, *to lead away, carry off.*
    Brīsēis, Brīsēidos, abl. **Brīsēide**, f., *Briseis* (Achilles' captive mistress in the Trojan war—for the name's Greek case endings, see on **Pēnēis** *Met.* I.472 above and cf. **Priamēide** 37 below).
    maestus, -a, -um, *unhappy, sad, sorrowful.*
    Achillēs, Achillis, m., *Achilles* (son of Peleus and Thetis, Greek prince in the Trojan war).
34   **dum licet**: we might say, *while you can* (which was not long, of course, as Troy was doomed to destruction, once Achilles returned to battle).
    Argēus, -a, -um, *Argive, of Argos* (an important city of the Greek Peloponnese); *Greek.*
    frangite, Trōes: for the epic apostrophe, cf. 24 above; the exhortation here adds a dash of emotion to Ovid's catalog of heroes.
    Trōs, Trōis, nom. and voc. pl. **Trōes**, m., *a Trojan.*
    opēs: here, *defenses* (a reference to the walls of the Greek camp at Troy).

35 **Hector, Hectoris**, m., *Hector* (the chief Trojan prince, eldest son of Priam and Hecuba).

Hector . . . arma: the famous scene of Hector's farewell to Andromache before rushing off to battle is in *Iliad* VI.

Andromachē, Andromachēs, f., *Andromache* (daughter of Eëtion and wife of Hector—the Greek case endings are the same as those of **Daphnē** and **Thisbē** above).

complexus, -ūs, m., *embrace, lovemaking*.

36 **galea, -ae**, f., *helmet*.

quae daret: a rel. clause of pupose, with **uxor** as antecedent; the prose order would be **uxor erat quae capitī galeam daret**, *he had a wife to place his helmet on his head* (an elaboration of Homer's account).

37 **summa ducum**: = **summus dux**, *the ultimate leader* (in apposition to **Atridēs**), but Ovid's substantive use of the n. pl. adj. is more striking, *the quintessence of leaders*.

Atridēs, Atridae, m., *son of Atreus* (king of the powerful Greek city of Mycenae, father of both Menelaus and, here, Agamemnon).

vīsā Priamēide: the abl. absolute is best translated as a temporal clause.

Priamēis, Priamēidos, abl. **Priamēide**, f., *daughter of Priam* (here, the prophetess Cassandra).

fertur: *is said*, + infin.

38 **Maenas, Maenadis**, f., *a Maenad, Bacchante* (a female devotee of Bacchus); *a frenzied woman*.

Maenadis . . . comīs: Cassandra resembled a Maenad as she wildly tossed her long, flowing hair in one of her oracular trances; the alliteration of **s** was perhaps meant to suggest the hissing of her frenzied prophetic utterances.

effūsus, -a, -um, *loose, flowing*.

effūsīs . . . comīs: dat. with the compound **obstipuisse**.

obstipēscō, obstipēscere, obstipuī, *to be stunned, dazed, awestruck* (here, in amazement at Cassandra's beauty).

39 **Mars . . . sēnsit**: Mars and Venus were caught in adultery by the goddess' husband, the blacksmith god Vulcan, who snared them in a bronze net and hung them on display for all the other Olympians to see and ridicule; Ovid tells the story in *Met.* IV, and see on *Am.* I.2.24 above.

dēprēndō, dēprēndere, dēprēndī, dēprēnsus, *to seize, catch; to catch in the act* (Mars, of course, was "caught" both literally and in this figurative sense).

dēprēnsus . . . sēnsit: placement of these two words at the caesura and line's end accentuates the assonance.

fabrīlis, -is, -e, *of a workman, an artisan's, a blacksmith's*.

40 **fābula nūlla fuit**: note the assonance with **fabrīlia vincula sēnsit** in the preceding line, especially the play on **fabrīlia/fābula**, both deliberately positioned to follow the caesura.

41 **Ipse ego**: the pronouns make an effective transition.

sēgnis, -is, -e, *inactive, lazy, sluggish*.

35 Hector ab Andromachēs complexibus ībat ad arma,
　　　et galeam capitī quae daret, uxor erat;
　　summa ducum, Atrīdēs, vīsā Priamēide, fertur
　　　Maenadis effūsīs obstipuisse comīs;
　　Mars quoque dēprēnsus fabrīlia vincula sēnsit—
40　　nōtior in caelō fābula nūlla fuit!
　　Ipse ego sēgnis eram discīnctaque in ōtia nātus;
　　　mollierant animōs lectus et umbra meōs.
　　Impulit ignāvum fōrmōsae cūra puellae

Discussion Question

What is the purpose of the four epic allusions in 33–40? How do they relate
to the ideas presented in 1–2 and 31–32? In what respects are the references
alike and in what ways do they differ? What significance do you see in the
order of presentation?

---

sēgnis: the word looks back to the charge of **dēsidia** in 31; in military
　　contexts, both **sēgnitia** and **dēsidia** implied dereliction of duty.
discīnctus, -a, -um, in *loose-fitting attire; easygoing, undisciplined.*
　　discīncta . . . ōtia: there is a military allusion here, as **ōtium** often
　　referred to the status enjoyed by one discharged from the army and the
　　adj. (here a transferred epithet) was used of soldiers who were
　　unarmed and had unbelted their tunics. Readers of Catullus might
　　compare his poem 51 on the perils of **ōtium**.
ōtium, -ī, n., often pl. for sing., *leisure.*
nātus: sc. **sum**; + **in**, *I was born for* or *I was naturally inclined to.*
42　**molliō, -īre, -iī, -ītus**, *to soften; to weaken.*
animōs . . . meōs: here, continuing the military metaphor in **animōs** (5), *my
　　fighting spirit*; note the internal rhyme (and cf. **castrīs . . . suīs** 44).
lectus et umbra: hendiadys, *my shaded lounge* (where the poet would often
　　recline to write his verse); **umbra** was a common metaphor for leisured
　　retirement (cf. our expression, "to have it made in the shade").
43　**Impulit ignāvum**: sc. **mē** here and with **iussit . . . merēre** (44).
cūra: subject of both **impulit** and **iussit**; with the objective gen. **puellae** the
　　word means *love* or *affection*, but the military double entendre is continued
　　(as is clear from **castrīs** 44), since **cūra** + the objective gen. often
　　referred to the command of an army or responsibility for some military
　　assignment.

44   **iussit et**: anastrophe.

    castrīs . . . suīs: the reflex. adj. here refers to **cūra** = **amor**; cf. **habet sua castra Cupīdō** (1).

    aes, aeris, n., *copper, bronze; money* (here with specific reference to the **aera mīlitāria,** *army pay*).

    mereō, -ēre, -uī, -itus, *to receive* (as a wage), *earn* (money).

        merēre: the verb was regularly used of earning money for sexual favors (hence the noun **meretrīx,** *prostitute*), a nuance doubtless intended here.

45   **vidēs**: with the 2nd pers. verb we are reminded of the poem's (rather generalized) addressee (Atticus, line 2).

    agilis, -is, -e, *swift, agile; active* (from **agere,** hence the opposite of **sēgnis** 41 and **dēsidiōsus** 46).

        agilem . . . gerentem: sc. **mē.**

    bella: *wars,* but perhaps with a play on the adj., *lovely (activities)*; cf. on **bella puella** (6).

46   **Quī . . . amet**: a final, stirring "call to arms," based on the arguments the poet has presented.

    dēsidiōsus, -a, -um, *idle, lazy* (cf. **dēsidiam** 31).

"Venus Awaits the Return of Mars"
Lambert Sustris, ca. 1570, Louvre, Paris

iussit et in castrīs aera merēre suīs:
45   inde vidēs agilem nocturnaque bella gerentem.
    Quī nōlet fierī dēsidiōsus, amet!

Discussion Questions

1.   Comment on the word-picture in 44.

2.   What is the function of the last three couplets (41–46)? What specific images does this section recall from earlier in the poem?

3.   How is this poem, in its structure and its argumentation, like a miniature speech of persuasion? Which lines constitute the prologue and epilogue, and what specific functions do those sections serve? What principal point does the speaker hope to prove? Summarize his major arguments. Are they convincing? Are they meant to be?

Briseis taken from Achilles
Pompeii, 1st century A.D.
Museo Archeologico Nazionale
Naples

1   ***colligō, colligere, collēgī, collēctus**, *to gather (together); to arrange.*
     Colligere . . . et . . . pōnere: construe both infinitives with **docta**, *skilled at.*
    incertōs: here, *disarrayed, disheveled.*
    *ōrdō, ōrdinis, m., *a row, line; social status, class; order, arrangement.*

2   **doctus, -a, -um**, *learned, wise; expert, skilled (at).*
     docta: this epithet and the series of adjectives and participles in each of the several phrases following (through **reperta** 5) are vocatives in agreement with **Napē**; calling the girl *learned* in this context adds a comic touch.
    neque . . . habenda: *and not one to be considered.*
    ancillās inter: anastrophe; Nape is no ordinary slave-girl, as we shall see.
    Napē, Napēs, f., *Nape* (the slave-girl in this little drama—she has a common Greek name, and the role she plays as go-between is typical of the maids in Roman comedy).

3   **ministerium, -ī**, n., *activity* (of a slave), *service; duty* (cf. **MINISTRĀS** 27).
    fūrtīvus, -a, -um, *stolen; secret, clandestine.*
     fūrtīvae: here, as often, a transferred epithet, logically referring to **ministeriīs**, but more imaginatively applied to **noctis**.

4   **ūtilis**: predicate adj. with **cognita** (3), *known (to be) useful (in)*; cf. **fīda reperta** (6). Note the identical, and emphatic, positioning of **docta** (2) and **ūtilis**; "intellect" and "pragmatism" are wonderfully complementary virtues!
    dandīs . . . notīs: the gerundive phrase is dat. of reference or purpose with **ingeniōsa**; for the internal rhyme, cf. 6, 12, and 28, and for the word order (modifier at caesura, noun at line's end), common in Ovid's pentameters, cf. 6, 8, 14, etc.
    ingeniōsus, -a, -um, *clever, gifted, talented (at).*

5   **saepe . . . / saepe** (6): the anaphora adds emotional intensity, as the past services Ovid recalls come nearer and nearer to the purpose of his request on the present occasion.
    hortāta: lit., *having urged*, but freely, *you who have urged*; in prose the verb takes an **ut** clause, but in verse an infinitive is common.
    Corinna, -ae, f., *Corinna* (the name of a Greek lyric poetess, used by Ovid for the mistress of his *Amores*).

6   **labōrantī . . . mihī**: dat. with **fīda** (cf. **FĪDĀS SIBI** 27); English would use a clause, not a participle, *whenever I was laboring* or *having difficulty* (in love).
    fīda: for the usage, see on **ūtilis** (4).
    reperta: freely (cf. **hortāta** 5), *(you who have been) found (to be).*

7   **accipe . . . / perfer . . . pelle** (8): the series of three imperatives (the first two in initial line position) stresses the urgency of the speaker's request.
    dominam: Corinna was both Nape's *mistress* and Ovid's.
    perarō, -āre, -āvī, -ātus, *to plow through; to incise, inscribe.*
    mane: with **perarātās . . . tabellās** (not **perfer**).
    *tabella, -ae, f., *a board, tablet;* pl., *writing tablet* (a common type of

AMORES I.11
"A Letter to Corinna"

Colligere incertōs et in ōrdine pōnere crīnēs
    docta, neque ancillās inter habenda, Napē,
inque ministeriīs fūrtīvae cognita noctis
    ūtilis, et dandīs ingeniōsa notīs,
5 saepe venīre ad mē dubitantem hortāta Corinnam,
    saepe labōrantī fīda reperta mihī,
accipe et ad dominam perarātās māne tabellās
    perfer, et obstantēs sēdula pelle morās.

Discussion Questions

1. How is the word order in verse 1 appropriate to the image described?

2. What is the rhetorical purpose of Ovid's lengthy characterization of Nape in 1–6?

3. How does the function of Nape as addressee differ from that of Atticus in *Am.* I.9?

4. If you are familiar with the poetry of Catullus, compare the function and organization of this poem's opening lines (1–7) with verses 1–16 of his poem 11. In what other respects are the two poems alike?

---

notebook, consisting of two boards with wax surfaces for inscribing messages with a stilus and hinged so that the tablet could be closed and sealed with the writing inside).

    tabellās / . . . morās (8): note the end-line rhyme and cf. 25–28; **morās** (*delays*) is deliberately "delayed," and **tabellās** in particular is emphatically placed, as it is (in the same case and number) in 15 and 25.

8 **perfer**: the prefix plays on **perarātās** (7) and has its full force here, *carry straight to* (i.e., straight through to the addressee without delay).

sēdulus, -a, -um, *attentive, careful* (here with adverbial force).

9   **Nec . . . nec . . . / nec** (10): anaphora intensifies the tricolon crescens.
    silicum: for the commonplace metaphor, cf. *Met*. X.242.
    vēnae . . . ferrum / . . . simplicitās (10): all are subjects of **adest** (sing. in
        agreement with the nearest of the three), with **tibi**, dat. of possession, *you
        have neither . . . .*

10 **simplicitās, simplicitātis**, f., *unity; simplicity; lack of sophistication,
    ignorance.*
        simplicitās ōrdine maior: *greater than (usual in) your class*. This point,
            like the next, seems a backhanded compliment—Nape is no more
            ignorant than others of her (low) social station! (Alternatively, as
            McKeown has suggested, one might accept the reading **et** for **nec** and
            take **simplicitās** in a positive sense, *integrity*, but this would undercut
            the anaphora, the tricolon, and, most importantly, the humor: Ovid
            pays more respect, as the drama develops, not to the maid but to his
            tablet!)

11 **crēdibilis, -is, -e**, *believable, credible, conceivable.*
        crēdibile est et tē: another backhanded compliment, *it is conceivable that
            even you* (have been in love)!
    et: = **etiam**.
    arcūs: metonymy for **sagittās**; for Cupid's bow and arrows, see *Met*.
        I.456-73 and *Am*. I.2.7-8.

12 ***mīlitia, -ae**, f., *military service.*
    signa: here, military *standards* (of the sort carried by Roman legions); for
        the military imagery cf. especially *Am*. I.9.
    tuēre: imper., *defend*; the point is that both Nape and Ovid are "soldiers" in
        the same army—Cupid's—and so each should look after the other's
        interests.

13 **quaeret**: Corinna is the understood subject.
    quaeret . . . dīcēs: note the aptly chiastic arrangement for query and reply;
        dīc might be expected in the apodosis, but **dīcēs** is more vivid.
    quid agam: idiom—not *what* but *how I am doing.*
    spē: abl. of means, but we would say *in hope.*
    noctis: not only *of the night* but also its pleasures (cf. **furtīvae . . . noctis**
        3).
    vīvere: sc. **mē** as subject of the indirect statement.

14 **cētera**: i.e., *other* (more intimate) *details* of his condition; the assonance in
        cētera/cēra, accentuated through positioning the words at the beginning of
        the verse and after the caesura, helps draw our attention to the shift of
        focus from Nape (**dīcēs**) to the tablet itself (**cētera fert . . . cēra**).
    blandā: transferred epithet; it is the message itself, rather than the hand that
        wrote it, which is *coaxing*, but Ovid's phrasing is more imaginative and
        more sensual.

15 **vacuae**: sc. **dominae**; i.e., approach her when she isn't busy.
    bene: in the sense of *quite* or *thoroughly*, the adv. may modify **vacuae**, or
        with **redde** it may be taken to mean *opportunely* or *in timely fashion*, or (as
        Kenney suggests) it may be taken in common with both words.

Nec silicum vēnae, nec dūrum in pectore ferrum,
10   nec tibi simplicitās ōrdine maior adest;
crēdibile est et tē sēnsisse Cupīdinis arcūs—
      in mē mīlitiae signa tuēre tuae.
Sī quaeret quid agam, spē noctis vīvere dīcēs;
      cētera fert blandā cēra notāta manū.
15   Dum loquor, hōra fugit—vacuae bene redde tabellās,
      vērum continuō fac tamen illa legat!
Aspiciās oculōs mandō frontemque legentis
      (et tacitō vultū scīre futūra licet).

Discussion Questions

1. How are 9–12 comparable in function to 1–5, and how do they differ?

2. Compare the speaker's comments to Nape in 11–12 with Orpheus' remarks to the gods of the Underworld in *Met.* X.27–29 above. How are the remarks similar in both content and purpose?

3. Comment on the multiple sound effects in verse 12.

4. How does meter suit meaning in line 15?

---

16   **vērum**, conj., *but*.
      continuō, adv., *immediately, without delay* (here with **legat**).
      fac . . . legat: i.e., **fac ut illa legat**, *see to it that she reads them*; a
        substantive volitive (or jussive noun) clause.
17   **Aspiciās . . . mandō**: = **Mandō ut aspiciās**, another volitive clause.
      oculōs . . . frontemque: take both with **legentis**, freely, *her eyes and face as*
        she reads.
      mandō, -āre, -āvī, -ātus, *to hand over, consign*; + **ut**, *to order, request*.
18   **et**: = **etiam**. Some editors favor the manuscript reading **ē**; but in addition to
      the other arguments for **et** is its contribution to the staccato sound effects
      (the alliterative **t**'s, the **et/licet** rhyme, and the assonant **-tō/-tū/-tū-**
      syllables, each under the ictus).
      tacitus, -a, -um, *silent, speechless*.
      scīre: with **licet**, *one may learn* (lit., *it is permitted to know*).
      futūrum, -ī, n., *the future*; pl., *future events*.

19 **Nec mora**: = **Sine morā**.

perlēctīs: sc. **tabellīs**, abl. absolute; again (cf. **perfer** 8) the prefix has its full intensive force (*thoroughly read*).

rescrībat . . . iubētō: = **iubētō ut rescrībat** (cf. **aspiciās . . . mandō** 17); the future imper. has a stern, legalistic tone, reminding us at once of poor Nape's humble rank and of the impropriety of her "ordering" her mistress to do anything (little surprise that Nape never responds through this entire drama, which is more a harangue than a dialogue).

20 **ōdī, ōdisse, ōsus**, defective verb with perf. forms and pres. meanings, *to have an aversion to, hate, dislike*.

   ōdī, cum lātē: the short words, hard consonants, and spondees pound out Ovid's indignation.

lātē, adv., *over a large area, largely, widely*.

splendidus, -a, -um, *bright, shiny; splendid, brilliant*.

21 **comprimō, comprimere, compressī, compressus**, *to compress, squeeze; to pack densely*; with **ōrdō**, *to close up* (the ranks of an army).

   Comprimat . . . morētur: chiasmus intensifies the hortatory verbs and neatly juxtaposes Corinna's (hoped-for) lines and Ovid's eyes.

ōrdinibus: sc. **in** and cf. **in ōrdine** (1)—Corinna's anticipated letter will be arranged in orderly fashion, just like her hair and like the soldiers in a Roman battalion. Nape's **simplicitās** is also "orderly"—see line 10—a very tidy poem in every respect!

versūs: here the *lines* of Corinna's letter.

oculōs . . . meōs (22): note the word-picture—Ovid's eyes are in fact *delayed*, not *at the margin's edge*, but at the extremities of the clause.

22 **extrēmus, -a, -um**, *at the edge, outermost*.

littera: Ovid often uses the sing. for an *epistle* and not just a letter of the alphabet (cf. *Am*. I.12.2 below). Ovid's switch from Corinna to the **littera** itself as subject anticipates his sharpening focus on the **tabellae** in the closing couplets.

****rādō, rādere, rāsī, rāsus**, *to scrape, scratch; to erase; to pass, move (closely) past*.

   rāsa: here probably *inscribed*, rather than *erased* (which, if correct, would imply a letter that Corinna had labored over, erasing and correcting). But McKeown's suggested emendation **arāta**, *inscribed*, is also attractive (cf. **perarātās** 7).

23 **digitōs . . . graphiō lassāre tenendō**: interlocked order; the entire infin. phrase complements **Quid . . . opus est**, *Why is it necessary*.

graphium, -ī, n., *stylus* (the Greek word for the Latin **stilus**, the pointed instrument used for writing on wax tablets).

lassō, -āre, -āvī, -ātus, *to make tired, tire, fatigue*.

24 **Hoc . . . scrīptum**: in apposition to **VENĪ**, which is set in capital letters here, just as Corinna might have written the word (and like the dedicatory inscription in 27–28).

scrīptum, -ī, n., *inscription; writing*.

tōta tabella, "VENĪ!": the highly alliterative verse and the strong diaeresis

Nec mora, perlēctīs rescrībat multa iubētō—
20   ōdī, cum lātē splendida cēra vacat!
Comprimat ōrdinibus versūs, oculōsque morētur
    margine in extrēmō littera rāsa meōs.
Quid digitōs opus est graphiō lassāre tenendō?
    Hoc habeat scrīptum tōta tabella, "VENĪ!"
25 Nōn ego victrīcēs laurō redimīre tabellās
    nec Veneris mediā pōnere in aede morer.

Discussion Questions

1. Why might we expect the epithet **victrīcēs** (25) to be applied to Nape? What is the effect of applying it instead to **tabellās**? What might we imagine as Nape's response? Why does she not respond?

2. In what several ways does Ovid gradually but emphatically shift his focus from Nape to the writing tablets in the second half of the poem (especially 15–26)?

following **tabella** prepare us for the brief message itself, which is suspended to line's end for further emphasis; Ovid pictures the single word inscribed in huge letters and filling the entire tablet.

25 **Nōn ego:** for this transition to the poem's closing section, cf. **ipse ego** (I.9.41).

victrīx, victrīcis, f. adj., *victorious;* (associated with or denoting) *victory.*

victrīcēs . . . tabellās: letters to the Roman senate announcing a military victory (the so-called **litterae laureātae**) were wreathed with laurel, but here the letter is itself pictured as *victorious*—a continuation of the military imagery in 21. For the laurel's association with triumphs and triumphant warriors, see the Daphne and Apollo story above, especially *Met.* I.558–61.

redimiō, redimīre, redimiī, redimītus, *to (encircle with a) garland, wreathe.*

redimīre . . . / nec . . . pōnere (26): complementary infins. with **morer,** a potential subjn.

tabellās / . . . morer / . . . MINISTRĀS / . . . ACER (28): note the ABAB end-line rhyme, one function of which (besides mere assonance) is to underscore the personifying link between **tabellās** and **ministrās.**

26 **aedēs, aedis,** f., *house; temple, shrine.*

27   **subscrībō, subscrībere, subscrīpsī, subscrīptus,** *to write at the bottom, append.*

    Subscrībam: possibly another potential subjn., but more likely a vivid future indicative, suggesting, along with the inscription following, the poet's heightened confidence in the success of his letter and the realization of his fantasy. Votive offerings to the gods were often accompanied by inscriptions on dedicatory **tabellae**—these were not usually love-letters, obviously, but this is Venus' temple, after all!

    FĪDĀS . . . MINISTRĀS: with these words the personification of the tablets, implied earlier, is now complete.

    Nāsō, Nāsōnis, m., *Naso* (Ovid's cognomen, with the final **-o** shortened here).

    ministra, -ae, f., *a female servant, maid.*

28   **dēdicō, -āre, -āvī, -ātus,** *to declare; to dedicate, consecrate (to).*

    DĒDICAT. AT: the abrupt diaeresis, harsh sound effects, and the unexpected adversative conjunction all prepare us for the poem's odd closure (which itself anticipates the following poem).

    NŪPER . . . ACER: internal rhyme further accentuates this final image. The tablets are alive; Ovid addresses them (**fuistis**); they have become his trusty maid-servants. But in this last curious flourish, he reminds these servants, as he had Nape, of their lowly station.

    vīlis, -is, -e, *cheap; worthless; contemptible; of inferior rank.*

    acer, acris, n., *the maple tree; maple wood.*

An ancient reader,
with writing implements,
from a Roman sarcophagus

Subscrībam, "VENERĪ FĪDĀS SIBI NĀSO MINISTRĀS DĒDICAT. AT NŪPER VĪLE FUISTIS ACER."

Discussion Question

What similarities of characterization, both positive and negative, do you see between the **tabellae** in 25–28 and Nape in 1–12? What is the dramatic effect of these associations?

Portraits (with tabella and scroll), Pompeii, 1st century A.D. Museo Archeologico Nazionale, Naples

1   **Flēte**: the pl. imper. immediately engages the audience.

      tristēs rediēre tabellae: the alliterative opening line makes it clear that this poem is a sequel—and a most unhappy one—to *Am.* I.11. And the vivid personification developed at the end of that poem bursts into action here: these tablets (not Nape) do the walking (**rediēre**) and the talking (**negat** 2)!

2   **īnfēlīx littera**: both *ill-omened* and *unproductive*, an elaboration of **tristēs . . . tabellae** (1); for the sing. form, cf. *Am.* I.11.22.

      posse negat: sc. **Corinnam** as subject of **posse** and **venīre** (from *Am.* I.11.24) as its complement.

3   **Ōmina**: the reference adds mock solemnity.

      aliquid: i.e., *something significant* (cf. the English idiom "that really is something!").

      cum discēdere vellet: **vellet** here serves essentially as an auxiliary, *when she was wanting to* (i.e., *was about to*) *leave*.

4   **ad līmen**: tripping was regarded as a bad omen by the Romans, but tripping *at a threshold* was even worse.

      digitōs: acc. of respect with the reflexive **icta**, *having stubbed her toes* (for the syntax, see on **ōra** *Met.* I.484 above).

      digitōs restitit icta: the alliteration has onomatopoetic effect.

5   **Missa . . . pedem** (6): regarded by some editors as an interpolation, this couplet is an effective apostrophe to poor Nape, who is ordered about and insulted, in absentia, just as she is in the preceding poem. For the opening participial phrase, English would use a clause, *Whenever you are sent*.

      līmen . . . pedem (6): the chiastic arrangement is appropriate to the action proposed, since it suggests a reversal of Nape's earlier, allegedly careless departure.

      meminī, meminisse, defective verb, *keep in mind, remember* (the fut. imper. here has the same stern tone as **iubētō** *Am.* I.11.19)

6   **cautē**, adv., *in a cautious manner, carefully* (both the enjambement, as McKeown observes, and the strong diaeresis suggest Nape's stumbling across the threshold).

      sōbrius, -a, -um, *not intoxicated, sober* (another humorously indelicate aspersion on Nape's character).

7   **Īte hinc**: the abrupt spondaic phrase, accentuated by elision and diaeresis, looks back to **rediēre** (1) and, following the prologue of 1–6, dramatically commences Ovid's curse.

      difficilēs: here, *troublesome, unhelpful*; the alliteration with **fūnebria** suggests Ovid's angry, hissing tone.

      fūnebria ligna: voc., in apposition to the enclosing phrase, **difficilēs . . . tabellae**; Ovid may mean that the tablet's wooden frame is good only for burning on a funeral pyre, but more generally the description anticipates the funereal images in 17–18.

      tabellae: cf. line 1; the poem's focal word is neatly set at the end of the first verse of each of the two principal sections (prologue and curse).

8   **tūque**: quite in the manner of ancient curses against persons, Ovid singles out the tablet's individual parts; cf. **vōsque** (14).

AMORES I.12

"Return to Sender!"

Flēte meōs cāsūs: tristēs rediēre tabellae;
    īnfēlīx hodiē littera posse negat.
Ōmina sunt aliquid: modo cum discēdere vellet,
    ad līmen digitōs restitit icta Napē.
5 (Missa forās iterum, līmen trānsīre mementō
    cautius atque altē sōbria ferre pedem!)
Īte hinc, difficilēs, fūnebria ligna, tabellae,
    tūque, negātūrīs cēra referta notīs,

Discussion Questions

1. How does the tone of the opening couplet (1-2) differ from the close of I.11? What key words in 1-2 set the tone, and where has Ovid positioned those words?

2. Why does Ovid make such a point about the **līmen** in 3-6? What symbolic function can the word have?

3. Comment on the word order and sound effects in **negātūrīs . . . notīs** (8) and compare the image with that of *Am.* I.11.24.

Ovid is the surest guide
    You can name, to show the way
To any woman, maid, or bride
    Who resolves to go astray.

"Written in an Ovid"
Matthew Prior

---

negātūrīs . . . notīs: cf. **littera . . . negat** (2).
refertus, -a, -um, *crowded, packed (with)*.

9   **puto:** the final **o** is shortened by systole (cf. on *Am.* I.2.5); the verb implies that this theory of the wax's origin is only Ovid's (spiteful) conjecture.

dē . . . Corsica (10): the prose order would be **dē flōre longae cicūtae sub melle īnfāmī collēctam;** the entire participial phrase modifies **quam,** object of **mīsit.**

longae . . . cicūtae: the adj./noun separation is appropriate to the image of the *long-stemmed hemlock.*

cicūta, -ae, f., *the hemlock plant.*

    Hemlock was the source of poison used in executions (notably that of Socrates), so that there is an allusion here comparable to those in 17–18; elsewhere (*Am.* III.7.13) Ovid refers to the drug's depressant effect on sexual drive, a further nuance probably intended here.

10   **mel, mellis,** n., *honey.*

melle . . . īnfāmī: Corsican honey was noted for its bitterness, which, together with the reference to poison here, accounts for the strong epithet; the honeycomb would be collected along with the honey but would settle to the bottom of the container, hence **sub.**

īnfāmis, -is, -e, *notorious, ill-reputed.*

Corsicus, -a, -um, *Corsican, of Corsica* (an island off Italy's west coast, noted for its honey, wax, and other exports).

mīsit: here, *exported,* sc. **Rōmam.**

apis, apis, f., *bee* (comically imagined here, with **mīsit,** shipping the wax and honey off to Rome all by itself!).

11   **At:** i.e., unlike Corsican wax.

minium, -ī, n., *cinnabar* (a substance used both as a source for red pigment and as a medication).

penitus, adv., *deep inside; deep(ly), thoroughly.*

medicātus, -a, -um, *treated, medicated (with); dyed (with).*

    In view of the context's references, not only to cinnabar, but also to death and poisoning, the word here means at once *colored* and *drugged;* cf. on **sanguinulentus** (12).

rubeō, rubēre, *to be(come) red; to blush.*

    The wax used for writing tablets was generally dark, and often had a reddish hue; but in view of the personification here, the better translation is *you were red-faced* (i.e., with guilt over your failure).

12   **ille:** here, like **iste,** in a pejorative sense.

sanguinulentus, -a, -um, *of blood, bloody; blood-red.*

sanguinulentus erat: the wax was crimson both with the "blood" that flushed its guilty face and, given the funereal associations of verses 7 and 17–18, with the blood of death.

13   **prōiciō, prōicere, prōiēcī, prōiectus,** *to cast forth, throw out.*

Prōiectae: sc. **tabellae,** voc. with the jussive **iaceātis;** English would more likely use two verbs, *may you be cast forth and lie . . . .*

trivium, -ī, n., often pl., *a crossroads.*

triviīs: sc. **in;** like our "street-corner" or "gutter," a place for worthless persons or things—and certainly not a charming final resting-place!

quam, puto, dē longae collēctam flōre cicūtae
10 melle sub īnfāmī, Corsica mīsit apis.
At, tamquam miniō penitus medicāta, rubēbās—
ille color vērē sanguinulentus erat!
Prōiectae triviīs iaceātis, inūtile lignum,
vōsque rotae frangat praetereuntis onus.
15 Illum etiam, quī vōs ex arbore vertit in ūsum,
convincam pūrās nōn habuisse manūs;
praebuit illa arbor miserō suspendia collō,

---

inūtilis, -is, -e, *useless* (contrast ūtilis, of Nape, in I.11.4 and ūsum 15
below).
    inūtile lignum: voc., in apposition to the understood tabellae, like
      fūnebria ligna (7) and cf. VĪLE . . . ACER (I.11.28).

14 vōsque: see on tūque (8).
    rotae: synecdoche for cart (cf. *Am.* I.2.42); Ovid wants us to focus on the
    wheel itself as it rolls over and shatters the tablet.
    praetereuntis: a slight echo of the identically placed pentasyllable
      sanguinulentus (12); in a message sent to Lesbia, Catullus (poem 11) uses
    the same word of a plow that crushes a flower in its path, a symbol of the
    love the poet's mistress has callously destroyed.
    onus: here the *weight* of a loaded cart.

15 Illum: subject of habuisse (16) in the indirect statement governed by
    convincam.
    quī . . . ūsum: i.e., the craftsman who made the tablet; in a poem Ovid has
    in mind here (*Odes* 2.13), Horace similarly curses both a tree that fell on
    him and the man who planted it.
    ūsum: here, *something useful*.

16 convincō, convincere, convīcī, convictus, *to overcome; to prove.*
    pūrās . . . manūs: this charge, that the carpenter was a villain, anticipates
    the tree's association with suicides and criminals in the next couplet.

17 praebuit illa . . . praebuit illa (18): careful positioning intensifies the
    anaphora.
    suspendium, -ī, n., *hanging* (i.e., death, especially suicide, by hanging;
    here, pl. for sing.).

18   **carnifex, carnificis**, m., *executioner*.
      dīrus, -a, -um, *grim, terrifying, horrible*.
      crux, crucis, f., *cross* (crucifixion was a common punishment for criminals).

19   **turpēs . . . umbrās**: through a chiastic word-picture (acc./abl./abl./acc.) the
      owls are enveloped by *loathsome darkness*; the epithets come first, holding
      the complete image in suspense to the end.
      raucus, -a, -um, *hoarse; raucous, noisy*.
        raucīs būbōnibus: both words are onomatopoetic, the latter especially
          (in its assonance with **umbrās**) suggesting the doleful moan of the owl.
      būbō, būbōnis, m., *eagle-owl, horned owl* (a bird of ill omen, like the
      vulture and the screech-owl in the following line).

20   **vultur, vulturis**, m., *vulture*.
      strix, strigis, f., *the screech-owl* (a mythic bird associated with vampires and
      ghouls).

21   **Hīs**: sc. **tabellīs** (cf. **hae . . . cērae** 23).
      ego . . . amōrēs: the interlocked order highlights the speaker's dismay.
      īnsānus, -a, -um, *crazed, insane*.

23   **capiant**: potential subjn., *would hold*.
      vadimōnium, -ī, n., *bond, recognizance* (a legal document guaranteeing a
      person's appearance in court—an irony here, in view of Corinna's message
      that she cannot honor Ovid's "summons").
      garrulus, -a, -um, *chatty, wordy*.
      cērae: i.e., **tabellae**.

24   **quās**: the word agrees with **cērae**, though **vadimōnia** is strictly the more
      logical antecedent.
      aliquis . . . ōre: interlocked order; **dūrō . . . ōre**, besides suggesting harsh
      legal language, is a deliberate play on **mollia . . . verba** (22). This
      criticism of legalistic language and maneuvering recalls Ovid's own
      rejection of the law as his profession.
      cognitor, cognitōris, m., *a legal representative, lawyer*.
      legat: subjn. by attraction to the imagined action of **capiant**; cf. **flēret** (26).

25   **inter . . . iacērent**: the quick dactylic rhythms of both this hexameter line
      and verse 23 help underscore the contemptuous tone of the two parallel
      couplets.
      ephēmeris, ephēmeridis, acc. pl. **ephēmeridās**, f., *a (daily) account book*.
      melius . . . iacērent: potential subjn., like **aptius . . . capiant** (23).
      tabulās: here, *account-books* or *ledgers*; the image, like many others in
      Ovid, is inspired by a passage from an earlier elegist (Propertius
      3.23.19–20).

26   **avārus, -a, -um**, *greedy, avaricious; miserly* (here used substantively).

27   **Ergō ego vōs**: the conj. and strong pronouns, especially the shift back to 2nd
      pers. address (contrast **hīs ego** 21), mark the transition to the curse's
      denouement.
      vōs . . . duplicēs: sc. **esse**, indirect statement with **sēnsī**.
      rēbus: abl. of respect; with **prō nōmine**, *in fact as well as in name*.

       carnificī dīrās praebuit illa crucēs;
    illa dedit turpēs raucīs būbōnibus umbrās,
20   vulturis in rāmīs et strigis ōva tulit.
    Hīs ego commīsī nostrōs īnsānus amōrēs
       molliaque ad dominam verba ferenda dedī?
    Aptius hae capiant vadimōnia garrula cērae,
       quās aliquis dūrō cognitor ōre legat;
25   inter ephēmeridās melius tabulāsque iacērent,
       in quibus absūmptās flēret avārus opēs.
    Ergō ego vōs rēbus duplicēs prō nōmine sēnsī—

Discussion Questions

1.   **Dīrās** is a widely accepted conjecture for the manuscript reading **dūrās** in verse 18. What several arguments can you think of both for and against the two readings?

2.   What specifically does Ovid curse in 9–12? in 13–20? How do these sections relate to 7–8?

3.   Comment on the imagery in 17–20. Where is this imagery first anticipated? How is it appropriate to the overall tone of the poem?

4.   What is the rhetorical function of 21–22? What is the emotional tone?

5.   How is Ovid's use of demonstrative pronouns in 12–23 especially effective?

6.   Comment on the word-picture in 23.

7.   What is the function of 23–26? In what ways do these lines have an affinity to satire?

8.   Explore fully the image of "doubleness" and "duplicity" evoked in line 27. In what ways does the image serve as a kind of metaphor for the entire drama contained in *Am.* I.11–12? Why is it especially appropriate that this drama be enacted in a diptych, rather than within a single poem?

duplex, duplicis, *double, folded over; two-faced, deceitful, duplicitous* (Ovid plays on both senses here, the literal and the figurative, a point which the interlocked order helps to underscore).

28 **auspiciī . . . bonī**: gen. of description in place of a predicate nom. after
erat; the chiastic golden-line arrangement (cf. **immundō . . . sitū** 30) suits
the image of the folding tablet itself.

29 **precer**: deliberative subjn.
nisi: sc. **ut**, *except that*, introducing a jussive noun clause after **precer.**
cariōsus, -a, -um, *decayed, rotten*.
senectūs, senectūtis, f., *old age* (a time of life devoid of love, as both Ovid
and the tablet must now be).

30 **rōdō, rōdere, rōsī, rōsus**, *to gnaw; to eat away, erode*.
immundus, -a, -um, *unclean, foul*.
situs, -ūs, m., *neglect, disuse; rot, mold*.

Medieval statue of Ovid
Liceo d'Ovidio
Sulmona, Abruzzi

auspiciī numerus nōn erat ipse bonī!
Quid precer īrātus, nisi vōs cariōsa senectūs
30   rōdat, et immundō cēra sit alba sitū?

Discussion Questions

1. Where else in the poem, besides verse 28, is there a reference to unfavorable omens? What are the functions of this repeated notion, both structurally and thematically?

2. Comment on the final image in 29–30. What do we see happening to the tablet itself and, on the symbolic level, to the "person" the tablet has become in Ovid's imagination? How does the reference to color function here? Where else in the poem does Ovid refer to the color of the wax, and what is the significance of the shift?

3. In what way does the little drama enacted in this poem affect our interpretation of the sentiment expressed in the closing line of I.11?

4. If you are familiar with Catullus' poetry, what elements does this poem have in common with his second sparrow poem (poem 3)?

1 **novum . . . Amōrum:** the alliteration of **m** and especially the assonance in
 -ovum/-ōrum/-ōrum add an aptly delicate sound effect.
 tener, tenera, tenerum, *soft, tender.*
 māter Amōrum: Venus, mother of Cupid (cf. 15 below), and the goddess
 who inspired Ovid's *Amores.*

2 **rāditur . . . meīs:** English would more likely use an active construction, *my
 elegies are moving closely round the final turning post,* a metaphor from
 chariot racing.
 ***elegī, -ōrum,** m. pl., *elegiac verses, elegies.*
   elegīs . . . meīs: poetry often omits the prep. **ab** in the abl. of agent
   construction; for the internal rhyme, a favorite Ovidian effect, cf.
   verses 4, 16, and 18, and note the soundplay between **-tima/mēta/me-**
   and **māter** in verse 1.

3 **Quōs:** here = **Eōs,** *These (elegies) I—a child of the Paelignian
 countryside—have composed.*
 ***Paelignus, -a, -um,** *Paelignian, of the Paelignians* (a tribe of central Italy).
 rūs, rūris, n., *country, countryside.*
 alumnus, -ī, m., *nursling, child; native* (here, with **hērēs** 5 and **eques** 6, in
 apposition to **ego**).

4 **nec . . . dēdecuēre:** a not immodest litotes, but perhaps also defensive, in
 view of criticism Ovid's erotic verse had brought him from some quarters.
 dēlicia, -ae, f., usually pl., *pleasure, delight, any pleasurable activity* (here
 Ovid's greatest pleasure—his poetry).
 dēdecet, dēdecēre, dēdecuit, *to disgrace, dishonor.*

5 **sī quid id est:** a self-deprecating aside, *if this is anything,* i.e., if his
 background is of any interest to his audience. This same line appears in
 Ovid's autobiographical poem, *Tristia* IV.10 (verse 7).
 proavus, -ī, m., *a great-grandfather; ancestor, forefather.*
 vetus . . . hērēs: while strictly modifying **hērēs,** the adj. logically applies to
 ōrdinis, *descendant of an ancient (equestrian) family.*
 hērēs, hērēdis, m., *successor, heir.*

6 **nōn . . . eques:** i.e., he was born an equestrian, not merely elevated to the
 rank as a consequence of wealth gained from the latest war; but, with an
 eye to the imagery of verses 2 and 18, Ovid means us to think of the literal
 meaning of **eques** (*horseman*) as well (see on **ārea** 18).
 turbō, turbinis, m., *a spinning top* (or other spinning object); *whirlwind*
 (here used figuratively).
 eques, equitis, m., *horseman; knight, equestrian* (a member of the wealthy
 Roman equestrian class).

7 **Mantua, -ae,** f., *Mantua* (a town in Cisalpine Gaul, birthplace of the poet
 Vergil).
 Vērōna, -ae, f., *Verona* (another city of Cisalpine Gaul, birthplace of
 Catullus).

8 **Paelignae . . . ego:** alliteration of hard **g** adds emphasis to Ovid's boast.

9 **honestus, -a, -um,** *honorable.*
 arma: here, as often, metonymy for *war.*

AMORES III.15

"And Now, Farewell to Love"

Quaere novum vātem, tenerōrum māter Amōrum:
    rāditur haec elegīs ultima mēta meīs!
Quōs ego composuī, Paelignī rūris alumnus—
    nec mē dēliciae dēdecuēre meae—
5 sī quid id est, usque ā proavīs vetus ōrdinis hērēs,
    nōn modo mīlitiae turbine factus eques.
Mantua Vergiliō gaudet, Vērōna Catullō;
    Paelignae dīcar glōria gentis ego,
quam sua lībertās ad honesta coēgerat arma,
10   cum timuit sociās anxia Rōma manūs.
Atque aliquis spectāns hospes Sulmōnis aquōsī

Discussion Questions

1. Comment on the appropriateness of the metaphor in line 2. How does the word-picture enhance the image?

2. What are the most striking sound effects in 4?

3. Comment on the word order in 7–8. What is the significance of Ovid's associating himself with Catullus and Vergil in particular?

---

10   **sociās . . . manūs**: note the word-picture, with *fearful Rome* "surrounded by" the *allied forces*; the Paeligni took a leading role in the Social War of 91–87 B.C.

        anxius, -a, -um, *uneasy, anxious.*

11   **hospes**: here, *visitor, traveler.*

        Sulmō, Sulmōnis, m., *Sulmo* (a town of the Paeligni—see on verse 3—and Ovid's birthplace, modern Sulmona).

        aquōsus, -a, -um, *abounding in water, well-watered* (here because of the region's many streams).

12   **moenia, moenium**, n. pl., *(defensive) walls*.
      campī: here, *its territory* (cf. **campō** 16).
      tenent: here, *encircle, protect*.

13   **Quae**: the antecedent is **vōs** (14), i.e., the **moenia**, synecdoche for the city of
      Sulmo itself.
      tantum: with **poëtam**, a deliberate contrast with **quantulacumque** (14); the
      line's initial spondees add weight to the characterization.

14   **quantuluscumque, -acumque, -umcumque**, *however small, tiny* (a massive
      word, extended by the elision with **estis**, for so tiny an image—doubtless a
      deliberate effect).

15   *****cultus, -a, -um**, *cultivated; beautiful; elegant*.
          Culte . . . cultī: the line's elaborate chiastic structure, its anaphora and
          assonance, and the quick dactylic rhythms all mark a transition to the
          poem's epilogue—a farewell to elegy, to its inspiring divinities Cupid
          and Venus (who are recalled from line 1), and to its Muse, along with
          an expression of confidence in the work's survival.
      Amathūsius, -a, -um, *Amathusian, of Amathus* (a town in Cyprus, Venus'
      birthplace).

16   **aurea . . . signa**: naturally the military standards carried by Venus and her
      conquering son are golden!
      campō: we should read the word both literally, looking back to **campī** (12),
      and figuratively, of the poet's *field* of literary interest; cf. the nearly
      identical double entendre in **ārea** (18).
      vellō, vellere, vulsī, vulsus, *to pull out, pull up*; with **signa**, *to pull up the*
      standards (of an army), i.e., as a signal to break up camp and move on.

17   **corniger, cornigera, cornigerum**, *having horns, horned*.
          Corniger . . . Lyaeus: according to a legend well-known from
          Euripides' *Bacchae*, Dionysus was born out of Zeus' thigh with the
          horns of a bull; he was frequently depicted in Roman art as a youth
          with bull's horns.
      increpō, increpāre, increpuī, increpitus, *to make a loud noise; to strike*
      noisily.
      thyrsus, -ī, m., *thyrsus* (a staff, tipped with a pine-cone, ivy, or grape-
      leaves, carried by Dionysus and his followers and often symbolizing, as
      here, poetic inspiration).
      Lyaeus, -ī, m., *Lyaeus* ("the Liberator," a cult-title of Dionysus/Bacchus,
      here in his role as inspirer of poets—cf. *Am.* I.2.47–48 above).

18   **ārea**: with a double entendre comparable to those in **campō** (16) and in
      eques (6), which is deliberately echoed by **equīs** in the same metrical
      position here, the word means both a *field* over which one might literally
      drive a team of horses and a *field of endeavor*. The same imagery is used
      by Ovid in his *Fasti* (IV.10), which, along with the *Metamorphoses*, he
      must have in mind here; work was begun on both these poems shortly after
      publication of the second edition of the *Amores*.
      magnīs . . . maior: the two epithets play on the imagery of size introduced
      in 12–14.

moenia, quae campī iūgera pauca tenent,
"Quae tantum" dīcet "potuistis ferre poētam,
quantulacumque estis, vōs ego magna vocō."
15 Culte puer puerīque parēns Amathūsia cultī,
aurea de campō vellite signa meō.
Corniger increpuit thyrsō graviōre Lyaeus:
pulsanda est magnīs ārea maior equīs.
Imbellēs elegī, geniālis Mūsa, valēte—
20   post mea mānsūrum fāta superstes opus!

Discussion Questions

1. How is word order appropriate to image in verse 16?

2. What metaphor introduced earlier in the poem is resumed in 18? How are the
    images alike and in what ways are they different? Compare also the
    similarities between verses 1 and 19. How do these connections contribute to
    the poem's unity?

3. Discuss Ovid's use of military imagery in this poem, including the brief
    mention in verse 6, the references to the Paelignians' role in the Social War,
    the allusions to Cupid and Venus, and the final characterization of his elegies
    as **imbellēs** (19). Compare the love/war imagery in other selections from the
    Amores which you have read.

4. How does Ovid's language here at the close of his final elegy (19–20)
    correspond with the last lines of his opening poem (*Am.* I.1.27–30)? What is
    the purpose of these correspondences?

---

19 **imbellis, -is, -e**, *not suited to war, unwarlike.*
>   **Imbellēs . . . valēte**: this closing farewell to elegy and Muse balances
>   the opening invocation of Venus as **māter Amōrum** (1).

>   **geniālis, -is, -e**, *of one's soul; jovial, genial.*
>>   **geniālis Mūsa**: not just *friendly (congenial) Muse*, but *soul-inspiring
>>   Muse*; in Roman belief, the **genius** was a man's soul, his spiritual
>>   essence, and the seat of his intellect and talent.

20 **mānsūrum . . . opus**: voc., in apposition to **elegī**; English would use a
    relative clause, in place of the participle, *work that will remain . . .*
>   **superstes, superstitis**, *surviving, alive* (here, neatly juxtaposed to **fāta**, the
>   poet's own *death*).

VOCABULARY

This vocabulary lists all words that appear in the running vocabularies with asterisks, and all other words that appear more than once in the text.

A

ā or ab, prep. + abl., *from*

abeō, abīre, abiī, abitūrus, irreg., *to go away*

absum, abesse, āfuī, āfutūrus, irreg., *to be away, be absent, be distant*

absūmō, absūmere, absūmpsī, absūmptus, *to use up; to wear out, exhaust*

accendō, accendere, accendī, accēnsus, *to kindle, ignite; to make hotter, intensify*

accipiō, accipere, accēpī, acceptus, *to receive, get, welcome*

ācriter, adv., *fiercely*

acūtus, -a, -um, *sharp, pointed*

ad, prep. + acc., *to, toward, at, near*

adeō, adv., *so much, to such an extent*

adeō, adīre, adiī, aditus, irreg., *to come to, approach*

adhūc, adv., *still, as yet*

admoveō, admovēre, admōvī, admōtus, *to move toward*

adsum, adesse, adfuī, *to be present, near*

adversus, -a, -um, *opposite (to), facing, turned toward*

āēr, āeris, m., *air*

afferō, afferre, attulī, allātus, irreg., *to bring, bring to, bring in*

agō, agere, ēgī, āctus, *to do, drive*

albus, -a, -um, *white*

aliquis, aliquid, *someone, something*

aliter, adv., *otherwise, differently*

alter, altera, alterum, *the other (of two), another, a second, the one*

altus, -a, -um, *tall, high*

ambō, ambae, ambō, *both*

amictus, -ūs, m., *mantle, cloak*

amīcus, -a, um, *friendly, loving; of a friend or lover*

amō, -āre, -āvī, -ātus, *to love, like*

amor, amōris, m., *sexual passion, love; pl., the object of love, a lover; a love affair*

Amor, Amōris, m., *Cupid (the god of love)*

amplector, amplectī, amplexus sum, *to embrace*

an, conj., *whether, or, if*

ancilla, -ae, f., *slave-woman*

anima, -ae, f., *air, breath; soul, life; spirit, ghost*

animus, -ī, m., *mind*

annus, -ī, m., *year*

ante, prep. + acc., *before, in front of*

aptō, -āre, -āvī, -ātus, *to place, fit*

aptus, -a, -um, *tied, bound; + dat., suitable (for)*

aqua, -ae, f., *water*

āra, -ae, f., *altar*

arbor, arboris, f., *tree*

arcus, -ūs, m., *a bow*

ārdeō, ārdēre, ārsī, *to burn, blaze*

arduus, -a, -um, *tall, towering; steep, precipitous*

ārea, -ae, f., *open space, area*

arma, -ōrum, n. pl., *arms, weapons*

armātus, -a, -um, *armed*

ars, artis, f., *skill*

artus, -ūs, m., *a joint of the body; arm, leg, limb*

arvum, -ī, n., *field*

asper, aspera, asperum, *rough, harsh (to the touch); wild, uncultivated*

aspiciō, aspicere, aspexī, aspectus, *to look at, observe; to consider, think about*

at, conj., *but*

āter, ātra, ātrum, *black, dark*

atque, conj., *and, also*

attollō, attollere, *to raise, lift up*

audāx, audācis, *bold*

audeō, audēre, ausus sum, *to dare*

auferō, auferre, abstulī, ablātus, irreg., *to carry away, take away*

augeō, augēre, auxī, auctus, *to increase*

aura, -ae, f., *a breath of air, a breeze*

aurātus, -a, -um, *golden*

aureus, -a, -um, *golden*

auris, -is, f., *the ear*

aurum, -ī, n., *gold*

auspicium, -ī, n., *omen, augury*

aut, conj., *or*

avis, avis, m./f., *bird*

B

bellum, -ī, n., *war*
bene, adv., *well*
blanditia, -ae, f., *flattery, alluring speech*; often pl. with sing. meaning
blandus, -a, -um, *coaxing, flattering; persuasive, enticing*
bonus, -a, -um, *good*
bōs, bovis, gen. pl. **boum,** m./f., *ox, cow*
bracchium, -ī, n., *the forearm*

C

cacūmen, cacūminis, n., *peak, top*
cadō, cadere, cecidī, cāsūrus, *to fall*
caedēs, caedis, f., *killing, slaughter; blood, gore*
caelum, -ī, n., *sky, heaven*
callidus, -a, -um, *expert, wise; clever, crafty*
campus, -ī, m., *plain, field*
canō, canere, cecinī, cantus, *to sing, chant; to sing about, celebrate*
capillī, -ōrum, m. pl., *hair*
capiō, capere, cēpī, captus, *to take, capture*
captīvus, -a, -um, *captured, captive*
captō, -āre, -āvī, -ātus, *to catch*
caput, capitis, n., *head*
carmen, carminis, n., *a ritual utterance, chant, hymn; a song, poem*
carpō, carpere, carpsī, carptus, *to pluck, gather; to tear at; to travel, pursue*
cārus, -a, -um, *dear, beloved*
castra, -ōrum, n. pl., *a military camp*
cāsus, -ūs, m., *a fall; mishap, misfortune, accident*
caterva, -ae, f., *crowd*
causa, -ae, f., *reason*
cēdō, cedere, cessī, cessūrus, *to go, proceed;* + dat., *to yield to, be inferior to*
celeber, celebris, celebre, *famous*
celer, celeris, celere, *quick, swift*
cērā, -ae, f., *beeswax, wax; a writing tablet*
Cerēs, Cereris, f., *Ceres (goddess of grain)*
certus, -a, -um, *certain*
cervīx, cervīcis, f., often pl. for sing., *the neck*
cessō, -āre, -āvī, -ātūrus, *to be idle, do nothing, delay*
cēterī, -ae, -a, *the rest, the others*

cingō, cingere, cīnxī, cīnctus, *to surround, encircle*
cithara, -ae, f., *lyre*
citus, -a, -um, *swift, rapid*
clāmō, -āre, -āvī, -ātūrus, *to shout*
coeō, coīre, coiī, coitus, irreg., *to come together, meet; to form an alliance*
cognōscō, cognōscere, cognōvī, cognitus, *to find out, learn, hear of*
cōgō, cōgere, coēgī, coāctus, *to compel, force*
colligō, colligere, collēgī, collēctus, *to gather (together); to arrange*
collum, -ī, n., *neck*
color, colōris, m., *color*
columba, -ae, f., *a pigeon, dove*
coma, -ae, f., *hair*
comes, comitis, m./f., *companion*
comitor, comitārī, comitātus sum, *to accompany*
committō, committere, commīsī, commissus, *to bring together, entrust*
commodus, -a, -um, *pleasant*
commūnis, -is, -e, *common*
cōmō, cōmere, cōmpsī, cōmptus, *to make beautiful, adorn; to dress, arrange, comb*
compōnō, compōnere, composuī, compositus, *to compose*
concha, -ae, f., *shellfish; shell, pearl*
concidō, concidere, *to fall down*
concipiō, concipere, concēpī, conceptus, *to receive; to conceive, develop; to express or compose (in words)*
coniunx, coniugis, m./f., *a spouse*
cōnstō, cōnstāre, cōnstitī, cōnstātūrus, *to take up a position, stand upon, stand firmly*
cōnūbium, -ī, n., often pl. for sing.; *marriage, wedding rites*
conveniō, convenīre, convēnī, conventūrus, *to assemble, meet;* + dat., *to be suited (to), befit, harmonize (with)*
cor, cordis, n., *heart*
cornū, -ūs, n., *an animal's horn, an object made of horn*
corpus, corporis, n., *body*
crēdō, crēdere, crēdidī, crēditus + dat., *to trust, believe*
creō, -āre, -āvī, -ātus, *to beget, create*
crēscō, crēscere, crēvī, crētūrus, *to be born, arise; to increase, change into (by growing); to grow, bud*

crīmen, crīminis, n., *charge, accusation; misdeed, crime*
crīnis, crīnis, m., *a lack of hair*; pl. or collective sing., *hair*
crūdēlis, -is, -e, *cruel*
cruor, cruōris, m., *blood* (from a wound); *slaughter.*
cultus, -a, -um, *cultivated; beautiful; elegant*
cum, prep. + abl., *with*
cum, conj., *when, since, whenever, although*
cūnctus, -a, -um, *all*
Cupīdo, Cupīdinis, m., *Cupid* (Venus' son and the god of physical love)
cupiō, cupere, cupīvī, cupītus, *to desire, want*
cūr, adv., *why?*
cūra, -ae, f., *care*
cūrō, -āre, -āvī, -ātus, *to look after, attend to*
currō, currere, cucurrī, cursus, *to run*
currus, -ūs, m., *a chariot*
cuspis, cuspidis, f., *sharp point, tip*
custōs, custōdis, m./f., *guard*

D

Daphnē, Daphnēs, f., *Daphne*
dē, prep. + abl., *down from, concerning, about*
dēbeō, -ēre, -uī, -itus, *to owe,* (one) *ought*
decet, decēre, decuit, *to adorn; to be right for* (+ acc.); impers., *it is right, suitable*
dēmittō, dēmittere, dēmīsī, dēmissus, *to let down, suspend*
dēmō, dēmere, dēmpsī, dēmptus, *to remove, take away; to cut off*
dēnsus, -a, -um, *thick, dense; frequent*
dēpōnō, dēpōnere, dēposuī, dēpositus, *to lay down, put aside, set down*
dēscendō, dēscendere, dēscendī, dēscēnsūrus, *to come* or *go down, climb down*
deus, deī, m., *god* (nom. and voc. pl., **deī, diī, dī**)
dextra, -ae, f., *right hand*
dīcō, dīcere, dīxī, dictus, *to say, tell*
diēs, diēī, m. (f.), *day*
difficilis, -is, -e, *difficult*
digitus, -ī, m., *finger*
discēdō, discēdere, discessī, discessūrus, *to leave, go away, depart*
discrīmen, discrīminis, n., *distinction*

diū, adv., *for a long time*
dīversus, -a, -um, *opposite; different; separate*
dō, dāre, dedī, dātus, *to give*
doceō, docere, docuī, doctus, *to teach*
doleō, -ēre, -uī, -itūrus, *to be sorry, be sad, hurt*
dolor, dolōris, m., *grief, pain*
domina, -ae, f., *mistress, lady of the house*
domus, -ūs, abl. **domō**, acc. pl. **domōs**, f., *house*
donum, donī, n., *gift*
dubito, -āre, -āvī, -ātus, *to be in doubt* or *uncertain* (with **an** + indirect question); *to waver, hesitate*
dūcō, dūcere, dūxī, ductus, *to lead, take, bring*
dum, adv. and conj., *while, as long as*
duo, duae, duo, *two*
dūrus, -a, -um, *hard, firm; harsh*
dux, ducis, m., *leader, commander, general*

E

ē, ex, prep. + abl., *from, out of*
ebur, eboris, n., *ivory*; by synecdoche, *an object made of ivory*
ecce, interj., *look! look at . . . !*
ego, pl. **nōs**, *I, we*
ēgredior, ēgredī, ēgressus sum, *to go out, leave, disembark*
elegī, -ōrum, m. pl., *elegiac verses; elegies*
enim, conj., *for*; with **sed**, *but in fact*
eō, īre, iī, itūrus, irreg., *to go*
equus, -ī, m., *horse*
ergō, conj., *therefore*
ēripiō, ēripere, eripuī, ēreptus, *to snatch from, rescue*
errō, -āre, -āvī, -ātūrus, *to wander, be mistaken*
et, adv. and conj., *and, also*
etiam, conj., *also, even*
Eurydicē, Eurydicēs, acc., **Eurydicēn**, f., *Eurydice* (wife of Orpheus)
excēdō, excēdere, excessī, excessūrus, *to go out, leave*
exeō, -īre, -iī, -itūrus, *to go out*
expallēscō, expallēscere, expalluī, *to grow pale*
extendō, extendere, extendī, extentūrus, *to hold out*

exstinguō, exstinguere, exstīnxī, exstīnctus,
to put out, extinguish

F

fābula, -ae, f., story
faciēs, faciēī, f., outward appearance; face;
shape, form
faciō, facere, fēcī, factus, to make, do
fallō, fallere, fefellī, falsus, to deceive,
trick; to disappoint
falsus, -a, -um, untrue, false; misleading,
deceptive
fāma, -ae, f., news, report; tradition, story
fateor, fatērī, fassus sum, to acknowledge,
admit, confess
fātum, -ī, n., prophecy; destiny, fate; Fate
(as a deity); doom, death (often pl. for
sing.)
fax, facis, f., torch
fēlix, fēlīcis, lucky, happy, fortunate
fēmina, -ae, f., woman
fera, -ae, f., wild animal, beast
ferō, ferre, tulī, lātus, irreg., to carry,
bring, bear
ferōx, ferōcis, fierce
ferrum, -ī, n., iron; by synecdoche, weapon,
sword
ferus, -a, -um, wild, ferocious, savage
festus, -a, -um, festive; with diēs (and often
pl.), a holiday, festival
fētus, -ūs, m., giving birth; fruit; offspring
fīdus, -a, -um, faithful, loyal, devoted
fīgō, fīgere, fīxī, fīxus, to drive in, insert; to
transfix, pierce; to fix, press
figūra, -ae, f., form, composition; outward
appearance
fīlia, -ae, f., daughter
fīlius, -ī, m., son
fīniō, -īre, -īvī, -ītus, to finish
fīnis, -is, m., end
fīō, fierī, factus sum, irreg., to become, be
made, be done, happen
flamma, -ae, f., flame
flāvus, -a, -um, yellow, fair-haired, blonde
flectō, flectere, flexī, flexus, to bend, curve;
to turn
fleō, flēre, flēvī, flētus, to weep, cry; to
weep for, lament
flōs, flōris, m., flower
flūmen, flūminis, n., stream, river
fōns, fontis, m., a spring, spring-water

forās, adv., out of doors, forth, out
foris, foris, f., door, entrance (of a building
or room); pl., double-doors
fōrma, -ae, f., form, shape; beauty
fōrmōsus, -a, -um, beautiful, lovely
fors, fortis, f., chance, destiny
fortis, -is, -e, brave
frangō, frangere, frēgī, fractus, to break
frōns, frondis, f., the leafy part of a tree,
foliage
frōns, frontis, f., forehead
frūstrā, adv., in vain
fuga, -ae, f., running away, flight
fugiō, fugere, fūgī, fugitūrus, to flee
fugō, -āre, -āvī, -ātus, to drive away,
dispel, banish
fūmus, -ī, m., smoke
fūnebris, -is, -e, funereal
fungor, fungī, fūnctus sum + abl., to
perform; to experience, suffer (with
morte and similar words, to die)
furor, furōris, m., frenzy

G

gaudeō, gaudēre, gāvīsus sum, to be glad,
rejoice
gelidus, -a, -um, cold, cool, chilly
geminus, -a, -um, twin-born, twin; twofold,
double
gemma, -ae, f., jewel, gem
genitor, -ōris, m., father, creator
gēns, gentis, f., family, clan
gerō, gerere, gessī, gessus, to wear, carry
on
glōria, -ae, f., fame, glory
grātus, -a, -um, pleasing, dear (to), loved
(by)
gravis, -is, -e, heavy, serious

H

habeō, -ēre, -uī, -itus, to have, hold
habitō, -āre, -āvī, -ātus, to live, dwell
haereō, haerēre, haesī, haesus, to stick,
cling; to be hesitant, be uncertain
hauriō, haurīre, hausī, haustus, to drain, to
draw in
herba, -ae, f., a small plant, herb; grass
hērōs, hērōos, m., hero
heu, interj., alas!

hic, haec, hoc, *this*
hīc, adv., *here*
hinc, adv., *from this place; from* or *on this side*
hodiē, adv., *today*
homō, hominis, m., *man*
hōra, -ae, f., *hour*
hortor, hortārī, hortātus sum, *to encourage, urge*
hospes, hospitis, m., *friend, host, guest*
hostis, hostis, m./f., *enemy*
hūc, adv., *here, to here*
hūmānus, -a, -um, *human*

I

iaceō, iacēre, iacuī, iacitūrus, *to lie, be lying down*
iaciō, iacere, iēcī, iactus, *to throw*
iam, adv., *now, already*
ibi, adv., *there*
īciō, īcere, īcī, ictus, *to strike*
īdem, eadem, idem, *the same*
ignāvus, -a, -um, *cowardly, lazy*
ignis, ignis, m., *fire*
ille, illa, illud, *that; he, she, it; that famous*
imber, imbris, m., *rain*
impellō, impellere, impulī, impulsus, *to strike, beat against; to motivate*
īmus, -a, -um, *lowest, bottommost; the bottom of, base of*; n. pl., substantive, *the Underworld*
in, prep. + acc. and abl., *into, toward, until; in, on, among*
incēdō, incēdere, incessī, incessūrus, *to march, go*
incertus, -a, -um, *not fixed; uncertain, doubtful; disarranged*
incola, -ae, m./f., *inhabitant, tenant*
incumbō, incumbere, incubuī + dat., *to bend over; to throw oneself (on), fall (on), lie down (on)*
inde, adv., *from there, then*
indignus, -a, -um, *unworthy (of), not deserving (to)* + infin.; *innocent*
indūcō, indūcere, indūxī, inductus, *to lead on, into*
inermis, -is, -e, *unarmed, defenseless*
īnfēlīx, īnfēlīcis, *unfertile, unproductive; disastrous, ill-fated, unfortunate*
ingenium, -ī, n., *intelligence, ingenuity*
ingēns, ingentis, *huge, big*

īnsequor, īnsequī, īnsecūtus sum, *to pursue, chase*
īnsula, -ae, f., *island*
inter, prep. + acc., *between, among*
intereā, adv., *meanwhile*
invītus, -a, -um, *unwilling, unwillingly*
ipse, ipsa, ipsum, *-self, very*
īra, -ae, f., *anger*
īrātus, -a, -um, *angry*
is, ea, id, *he, she, it; this, that*
iste, ista, istud, *that, that . . . of yours*
iter, itineris, n., *journey, road, path, way*
iterum, adv., *again, a second time*
iubeō, iubēre, iussī, iussus, *to order, bid*
iūgerum, -ī, n., *a measure of land*; pl., *an expanse of land, fields, acres*
iungō, iungere, iūnxī, iūnctus, *to join*
iūs, iūris, n., *law, legal sanction; legal authority, right*
iuvenis, iuvenis, m., *young man*

L

labor, labōris, m., *work, toil*
lābor, lābī, lāpsus sum, *to slip, stumble*
labōrō, -āre, -āvī, -ātūrus, *to work*
lacertus, -ī, m., *the arm*, especially *the upper arm*
lacrima, -ae, f., *tear*
laedō, laedere, laesī, laesus, *to harm, hurt, wound*
laetus, -a, -um, *happy, glad, joyful*
laniō, -āre, -āvī, -ātus, *to wound savagely; to tear, shred, mutilate*
lapis, lapidis, m., *stone*
lateō, latēre, latuī, *to lie in hiding, hide*
laudō, -āre, -āvī, -ātus, *to praise*
laurus, -ī, f., *a laurel tree, bay; a sprig or branch of laurel; a garland of laurel*
laus, laudis, f., *praise, reputation; praiseworthy act, honor*
lectus, -ī, m., *bed, couch*
legō, legere, lēgī, lēctus, *to gather, collect, select; to read*
leō, leōnis, m., *lion*
lepus, leporis, m., *rabbit*
lētum, -ī, n., *death, destruction*
levis, -is, -e, *light* (in weight); *nimble; gentle; unsubstantial, thin*
lēx, lēgis, f., *law; rule, regulation, order*
licet, licēre, licuit, impers., + dat., *it is allowed*

lignum, -ī, n., *firewood; wood; a stump; a shaft*

līmen, līminis, n., *threshold, doorway*

littera, -ae, f., *letter* (of the alphabet); pl., *letter, epistle, literature*

locus, -ī, m. (pl., *loca*, -ōrum, n.), *place*

longus, -a, -um, *long*

loquor, loquī, locūtus sum, *to speak, talk*

luctor, luctārī, luctātus sum, *to wrestle; to struggle, resist*

lūmen, lūminis, n., *light; an eye* (especially pl.), *vision, gaze, glance* (sing. or pl.)

lupus, -ī, m., *wolf*

lūx, lūcis, f., *light*

lyra, -ae, f., *a lyre*

M

magis, comp. adv., *more*

magnificus, -a, -um, *magnificent*

magnus, -a, -um, *big, great*

maneō, manēre, mānsī, mānsūrus, *to remain, stay*

manus, -ūs, f., *hand; band* (of men)

margō, marginis, m., *wall; border, edge; margin*

marītus, -ī, *husband*

Mars, Martis, m., *Mars* (Roman god of war)

māter, mātris, f., *mother*

māteria, -ae, f., *wood* (as a building material); *material, subject-matter*

medicīna, -ae, f., *medicine*

medius, -a, -um, *mid-, middle of*

membrum, -ī, n., *a part of the body, limb, member*

mēns, mentis, f., *the mind*

mēta, -ae, f., *mark, goal, turning-point*

metuō, metuere, metuī, metūtus, *to fear, be afraid of*

metus, -ūs, m., *fear*

meus, -a, -um, *my, mine*

micō, micāre, micuī, *to move quickly to and fro, flash*

mīles, mīlitis, m., *soldier*

mīlitia, -ae, f., *military service*

mīlle, indecl. adj., *thousand*

Minerva, -ae, f., *Minerva* (goddess of wisdom and warfare)

mīror, mīrārī, mīrātus sum, *to wonder*

mīrus, -a, -um, *wonderful, marvelous, strange*

misceō, miscēre, miscuī, mixtus, *to mix*

miser, misera, miserum, *unhappy, miserable, wretched*

miserābilis, -is, -e, *miserable, wretched*

mittō, mittere, mīsī, missus, *to send, let go*

moderātus, -a, -um, *temperate, moderate, restrained*

modo, adv., *only recently, just now;* modo . . . modo, *at one time . . . at another*

modus, -ī, m., *way, method*

mollis, -is, -e, *soft, tender; gentle*

moneō, monēre, monuī, monitus, *to advise, warn*

mōns, montis, m., *mountain, hill*

mora, -ae, f., *delay*

morior, morī, mortuus sum, *to die*

moror, morārī, morātus sum, *to delay, remain, stay*

mors, mortis, f., *death*

morsus, -ūs, m., *bite* (of an animal); pl., by metonymy, *teeth, jaws*

moveō, movēre, mōvī, mōtus, *to move, shake*

mox, adv., *soon, presently*

multus, -a, -um, *much;* pl. *many*

mūnus, mūneris, n., *a required task; tribute, offering* (to a deity); *gift* (with prō, *as a gift); favor, service*

murmur, murmuris, n., *murmur, ramble*

mūrus, -ī, m., *wall*

mūtō, -āre, -āvī, -ātus, *to exchange; to change, replace; to transform*

myrtus, -ī, m./f., *myrtle*

N

nam, conj., *for*

narrō, -āre, -āvī, -ātus, *to tell* (a story)

nāscor, nāscī, nātus sum, *to be born*

nātūra, -ae, f., *nature*

nē, conj. (+ subjn.), *in case, to prevent, not to*

nec, conj., *and . . . not*

negō, -āre, -āvī, -ātus, *to say (that) not; to refuse*

neque, conj., *and . . . not*

nēquīquam, adv., *with no effect, to no avail, in vain*

nervus, -ī, m., *a muscle, nerve; a cord* (made of such material), *string* (of a musical instrument or a bow)

nesciō, -īre, -īvī, -ītus, *to be ignorant, not know*

nex, necis, f., *death, murder*

nīl, n., indecl., *nothing*

nimis, adv., *too much*

nimium, adv., *too much, excessively*

nisi, conj., *unless, if . . . not, except*

niveus, -a, -um, (consisting) *of snow; snow-white, snowy*

nix, nivis, f., *snow*

noceō, -ēre, -uī, -itūrus + dat., *to harm*

nocturnus, -a, -um, *happening during the night*

nōlō, nōlle, nōluī, irreg., *to be unwilling, not wish, refuse*

nōmen, nōminis, n., *name*

nōminō, -āre, āvī, -ātus, *to name, call by name*

nōn, adv., *not*

nōndum, adv., *not yet*

noster, nostra, nostrum, *our*

notō, -āre, -āvī, -ātus, *to mark, brand; to scar; to notice; to inscribe*

nōtus, -a, -um, *known*

novus, -a, -um, *new*

nox, noctis, f., *night*

nūllus, -a, -um, *no, none*

nūmen, nūminis, n., *a nod* (of assent); *divine power, supernatural influence*

numerō, -āre, -āvī, -ātus, *to count*

numerus, -ī, n., *number*

nunc, adv., *now*

nūper, adv., *recently*

O

ō, interj., *oh!*

obscūrus, -a, -um, *dark, obscure; shadowy; hidden from sight*

observō, -āre, -āvī, -ātus, *to watch, pay attention to*

obsideō, obsidēre, obsēdī, obsessus, *to besiege*

obstō, obstāre, obstitī, obstātūrus + dat., *to face; to stand in the way (of); obstruct*

occupō, -āre, -āvī, -ātus, *to seize*

ōcior, ōcior, ōcius, compar. adj., *swifter, more fleeting*

oculus, -ī, m., *eye*

officium, -ī, n., *official ceremony, duty*

ōlim, adv., *once (upon a time), one day*

ōmen, ōminis, n., *omen, augury, sign*

omnis, -is, -e, *all, the whole, every, each*

onus, oneris, n., *load, burden*

opācus, -a, -um, *shaded; shadowy, dark, dim*

ops, opis, f., *power, ability; resources; aid*

optō, -āre, -āvī, -ātus, *to wish*

opus, operis, n., *work, task; function, purpose;* **opus est** + abl., idiom, *there is need of* (something)

ōra, -ae, f., *shore, coast*

orbis, orbis, m., *a disc, any disc-shaped object; wheel; orb* (of the sun or moon); *the world*

ōrdō, ōrdinis, m., *a row, line; social status, class; order, arrangement*

ōrnō, -āre, -āvī, -ātus, *to decorate, equip*

ōrō, -āre, -āvī, -ātus, *to beg*

ōs, ōris, n., *mouth, face, expression* (pl. common for s. in verse)

os, ossis, n., *bone*

ōsculum, -ī, n., *little mouth;* (most commonly) *a kiss* or, pl., *lips*

ōvum, -ī, n., *egg*

P

Paelignus, -a, -um, *Paelignian, of the Paelignians* (a tribe of central Italy)

parcō, parcere, pepercī + dat., *to spare*

parēns, parentis, m./f., *parent*

pariēs, parietis, m., *wall*

parō, -āre, -āvī, -ātus, *to prepare*

pars, partis, f., *part*

parvus, -a, -um, *small*

passus, -ūs, m., *step, pace, stride*

pateō, -ēre, -uī, *to be open; to be visible, revealed*

pater, patris, m., *father*

patior, patī, passus sum, *to suffer, endure*

paucī, -ae, -a, *few*

paulum, adv., *a little, little*

pāx, pācis, f., *peace*

pectus, pectoris, n., *chest, breast*

pellō, pellere, pepulī, pulsus, *to beat against, strike; to drive away, banish, expel*

pendeō, pendēre, pependī, *to be suspended, hang; to hang down* (upon or over)

Pēnēis, Pēnēidos, abl. sing. **Pēnēide,** voc. sing. **Pēnēi,** acc. pl. **Pēnēidas,** *of the river Peneus, descended from the river-god Peneus*

Pēnēius, -a, -um, *of Peneus, child of Peneus*

penna, -ae, f., *a wing; a feather*

per, prep. + acc., *through, along, over*

peragō, peragere, perēgī, perāctus, *to chase; to complete; to go through* (space or time); *to live out, complete* (a period of time)

percutiō, percutere, percussī, percussus, *to strike; to beat, shake violently*

perdō, perdere, perdidī, perditus, *to destroy, ruin; to waste*

perferō, perferre, pertulī, perlātus, irreg., *to report; to endure, to carry* (to someone)

perīculum, -ī, n., *danger*

perlegō, perlegere, perlēgī, perlēctus, *to read through*

perveniō, pervenīre, pervēnī, perventūrus, + ad + acc., *to arrive (at), reach*

pēs, pedis, m., *foot*

petō, petere, petīvī, petītus, *to seek, look for, aim at, attack*

pharetra, -ae, f., *quiver*

Phoebē, -ēs, f., *Diana* (sister of Phoebus Apollo and virgin goddess of the moon)

Phoebus, -ī, m., *Phoebus* (Apollo, god of the sun and the arts)

pila, -ae, f., *ball*

placeō, placēre, placuī, placitus + dat., *to please*

plēnus, -a, -um, *full*

plumbum, -ī, n., *lead*

poēta, -ae, m., *poet*

pollex, pollicis, m., *thumb*

polliceor, pollicērī, pollicitus sum, *to promise*

pompa, -ae, f., *a ceremonial procession*

pōmum, -ī, n., *fruit-tree; fruit*

pōnō, pōnere, posuī, positus, *to put, place*

populus, -ī, m., *people*

porta, -ae, f., *gate*

portō, -āre, -āvī, -ātus, *to carry*

poscō, poscere, poposcī, *to ask for, demand*

possum, posse, potuī, irreg., *to be able*

post, prep. + acc., *after*

posterus, -a, -um, *next, following*

postis, -is, m., *door-post*

postquam, conj., *after*

potentia, -ae, f., *power, potency*

praebeō, -ēre, -uī, -itus, *to display, show, provide*

praeda, -ae, f., *booty, plunder; prey, game*

praeferō, praeferre, praetulī, praelātus, irreg., *to carry in front, prefer*

praetereō, praeterīre, praeteriī, praeteritus, irreg., *to go past*

precor, -ārī, -ātus sum, *to pray for, beg*

premō, premere, pressī, pressus, *to press, press upon; to cover; to oppress*

prēndō, prēndere, prēndī, prēnsus, *to grasp, seize, take hold of; to catch, capture*

prīmum, adv., *first, at first*

prīmus, -a, -um, *first*

prior, prius, *first* (of two), *previous*

procul, adv., *in the distance, far off*

prōnus, -a, -um, *face down*

properō, -āre, -āvī, -ātus, *to act with haste, be quick; to hurry, rush*

prōsum, prōdesse, prōfuī + dat., irreg., *to be of use to, benefit, help*; + infin., *to be beneficial* (to do something)

prōtinus, adv., *immediately*

pudor, pudōris, m., *sense of shame; decency, chastity*

puella, -ae, f., *girl*

puer, -ī, m., *boy*

pulcher, pulchra, pulchrum, *beautiful, handsome*

pulsō, -āre, -āvī, ātus, *to strike, beat*

pūrus, -a, -um, *spotless, clean*

putō, -āre, -āvī, -ātus, *to think, consider*

Pygmaliōn, Pygmaliōnis, m., *Pygmalion* (a sculptor from Cyprus)

Pȳramus, -ī, m., *Pyramus* (a Babylonion youth)

Q

quaerō, quaerere, quaesīvī, quaesītus, *to seek, look for, ask* (for)

quantus, -a, -um, *how big . . . ? how much . . . ?*

queror, querī, questus sum, *to complain (about), protest*

quī, quae, quod, *who, which, that*

quīcumque, quaecumque, quodcumque, indefinite adj. or pron., *whoever, whatever*

quid, adv., *why?*

quidem, adv., *indeed*

quīnque, indecl., *five*

quis, quid, pron., *who . . . ? what . . . ?*

quisque, quaeque, quidque, each
quisquis, quidquid, indefinite rel. pron.,
 any who, whoever, whatever
quoniam, conj., *since*
quoque, adv., *also*

R

radius, -ī, m., *a ray of light*
rādīx, rādīcis, f., *root* (of a plant or tree)
rādō, rādere, rāsī, rāsus, *to scrape,
 scratch; to erase; to pass, move (closely)
 past*
rāmus, -ī, m., *branch*
recēns, recentis, *recent, newly arrived;
 newly shed; recently caught*
recipiō, recipere, recēpī, receptus, *to
 receive*
reddō, reddere, reddidī, redditus, *to give
 back, return*
redeō, redīre, rediī, reditūrus, irreg., *to
 return, go back*
referō, referre, rettulī, relātus, irreg., *to
 bring back*
rēgia, -ae, f., *palace, royal house*
rēgnō, -āre, -āvī, -ātus, *to rule, govern,
 reign*
rēgnum, -ī, n., *kingdom*
regō, regere, rēxī, rēctus, *to rule*
relinquō, relinquere, relīquī, relictus, *to
 leave*
removeō, removēre, remōvī, remōtus, *to
 remove, move aside*
reperiō, reperīre, repperī, repertus, *to
 find, discover; to find (someone,
 something) to be*
**requiēscō, requiēscere, requiēvī,
 requiētūrus**, *to rest, lie at rest*
rēs, reī, f., *thing, matter, situation*
rescrībō, rescrībere, rescrīpsī, rescrīptus,
 to write back; reply
resistō, resistere, restitī, *to pause in one's
 journey, halt, stop*
**respondeō, respondēre, respondī,
 respōnsūrus**, *to reply*
retrō, adv., *toward the rear, backwards,
 behind*
revocō, -āre, -āvī, -ātus, *to recall, call back*
Rhodopēius, -a, -um, *of Mt. Rhodope* (in
 Thrace)
rīdeō, rīdēre, rīsī, rīsūrus, *to laugh, smile*
rīma, -ae, f., *crack*

rogō, -āre, -āvī, -ātus, *to ask*
Rōma, -ae, f., *Rome*
rosa, -ae, f., *rose*
rota, -ae, f., *wheel*
rumpō, rumpere, rūpī, ruptus, *to burst*
rūrsus, adv., *again*

S

sacer, sacra, sacrum, *sacred, religious*
saepe, adv., *often*
saevus, -a, -um, *fierce, savage*
sagitta, -ae, f., *arrow*
sanguis, sanguinis, m., *blood*
satis, adv., *enough*
saxum, -ī, n., *a stone, rock, boulder*
scindō, scindere, scidī, scissus, *to cut, split,
 carve*
sciō, scīre, sciī, scītus, *to know*
sē or (**sēsē**, acc. and abl.), gen. **suī**, dat.
 sibi, *himself, herself, oneself, itself,
 themselves*
sed, *but*
sedeō, sedēre, sēdī, sessūrus, *to sit*
sēdēs, sēdis, f., *seat; home; place, position*
semper, adv., *always*
senex, senis, m., *old man*
septem, indecl., *seven*
sepulcrum, -ī, n., *tomb*
sequor, sequī, secūtus sum, *to follow*
sērō, adv., *late*
serpēns, serpentis, m., *snake, serpent*
servō, -āre, -āvī, -ātus, *to save, keep,
 protect*
sex, indecl., *six*
sī, conj., *if*
sīc, *thus, in this way*
sīdus, sīderis, n., *a star planet; usually pl.,
 the stars*
signum, -ī, n., *signal, sign*
silentium, -ī, n., *silence*
silex, silicis, m., *hard stone, flint*
silva, -ae, f., *woods, forest*
similis, -is, -e, *like, similar (to)*
simul, adv., *together, at the same time*
simulācrum, -ī, n., *likeness; image, statue;
 phantom, ghost*
simulō, -āre, -āvī, -ātus, *to pretend; to
 produce, simulate*
sine, prep. + abl., *without*
sinō, sinere, sīvī, situs, *to allow*
sitis, sitis, acc. **sitim**, f., *thirst*

socius, -a, -um, *keeping company* (with another), (in the role of) *companion; allied*

sōl, sōlis, m., *the sun; Sol* (god of the sun)

sōlus, -a, -um, *alone*

somnium, -ī, n., *dream*

somnus, -ī, m., *sleep*

spargō, spargere, sparsī, sparsus, *to scatter, strew; to allow to stream out*

spectō, -āre, -āvī, -ātus, *to watch, look at*

spērō, -āre, -āvī, -ātus, *to hope*

spēs, speī, f., *hope*

stō, stāre, stetī, statūrus, *to stand*

strātum, -ī, n., *bedding, coverlet;* (often in pl.) *bed*

strēnuus, -a, -um, *active, energetic*

stringō, stringere, strīnxī, strictus, *to bind, secure; to draw tight; to draw close to, touch*

stupeō, -ēre, -uī, -itus, *to be amazed, gape; to be paralyzed*

sub, prep. + acc. and abl., *under, beneath*

sum, esse, fuī, futūrus, irreg., *to be*

summus, -a, -um, *very great, the greatest, the top of*

superbus, -a, -um, *proud, arrogant*

superus, -a, -um, *above, upper*

surgō, surgere, surrēxī, surrēctus, *to get up, rise*

surripiō, surripere, surripuī, surreptus, *to steal*

sustineō, sustinēre, sustinuī, *to hold up, support; to sustain;* (+ infin.) *to be able* (to do something) *without relenting*

suus, -a, -um, *his, her, its, their (own)*

T

tabella, -ae, f., *a board, tablet;* pl., *writing tablet*

tabulae, -ārum, f. pl., *tablets, records*

taeda, -ae, f., *torch*

tālis, -is, -e, *such, like this, of this kind*

tam, adv., *so*

tamen, conj., *however, nevertheless*

tamquam, adv., *just as, as if, as though*

tandem, adv., *at last, at length*

tangō, tangere, tetigī, tāctus, *to touch*

tantus, -a, -um, *so great, such a big*

tardus, -a, -um, *slow*

tegō, tegere, tēxī, tēctus, *to cover; to hide, conceal*

tellūs, tellūris, f., *land, earth*

temerārius, -a, -um, *rash, reckless, bold*

temptō, -āre, -āvī, -ātus, *to try*

tempus, temporis, n., *time*

tendō, tendere, tetendī, tentus, *to extend, stretch forth; to proceed*

teneō, tenēre, tenuī, tentus, *to hold*

tenuis, -is, -e, *slender, thin*

tepeō, tepēre, tepuī, *to be warm; to have the warmth of a human body*

tergum, -ī, n., *back, rear*

terra, -ae, f., *earth, ground*

Thisbē, Thisbēs, f., *Thisbe* (a Babylonian maiden)

tigris, tigris, m./f., *tiger*

timeō, -ēre, -uī, -itūrus, *to fear*

timidus, -a, -um, *fearful, timorous*

timor, timōris, *fear*

tingō, tingere, tīnxī, tīnctus, *to wet, soak, moisten; to dye, stain, color*

tollō, tollere, sustulī, sublātus, *to lift, raise*

torus, -ī, m., *couch*

tot, indecl. num. adj., *so many*

tōtus, -a, -um, *all, the whole*

trahō, trahere, trāxī, tractus, *to drag, pull*

trānseō, trānsīre, trānsiī, trānsitūrus, irreg., *to cross*

tremō, tremere, tremuī, *to tremble*

trepidō, -āre, -āvī, -ātus, *to panic; to tremble, quiver*

trēs, trēs, tria, *three*

tristis, -is, -e, *sad*

triumphus, -ī, m., *the ritual shout "triumphe"; a triumph; a victory celebration; a victory*

tū, pl. vōs, *you*

tueor, tuērī, tuitus sum, *to look at, observe; to watch over, protect*

tum, adv., *at that moment, then*

tumidus, -a, -um, *swollen; enraged, violent*

tumulus, -ī, m., *burial mound, tomb*

turba, -ae, f., *crowd, mob*

turpis, -is, -e, *offensive, foul, disgusting; shameful, disgraceful*

tūtus, -a, -um, *safe, secure*

tuus, -a, -um, *your* (sing.)

U

ubi, *where, when*

ultimus, -a, -um, *last*

umbra, -ae, f., *shadow, shade* (of the dead)

umquam, adv., *ever*

unda, -ae, f., *wave, water*

ūnus, -a, -um, *one*

urbs, urbis, f., *city*

urgeō, urgēre, ursī, *to press, insist*

urna, -ae, f., *a pitcher, urn*

ūrō, ūrere, ussī, ustus, *to destroy by fire, burn*

ūsque, adv., *all the way to* or *from; continuously*

ūsus, -ūs, m., *use, employment; the right to use* or *enjoy; potential for use, utility; marriage*

ut, conj. + indicative, *as, when;* + subjunctive, *so that, that, to*

uterque, utraque, utrumque, *each* (of two), *both*

ūtilis, -is, -e, *useful*

uxor, uxōris, f., *wife*

V

vacō, -āre, -āvī, -ātus, *to be empty, unfilled; to be free from, take a rest from*

vacuus, -a, -um, *empty, hollow; carefree, fancy-free;* + abl., *devoid (of), free (from)*

valeō, -ēre, -uī, *to be strong, be well*

vapor, vapōris, m., *steam*

vātēs, vātis, m., *prophet; bard, poet*

vel, conj. and adv., *or, if you prefer, at least*

vēlāmen, vēlāminis, n., *veil, shawl,*

vēna, -ae, f., *blood-vessel, vein; vein, streak* (of some stone or mineral)

venia, -ae, f., *favor, kindness, blessing ; forgiveness, pardon; reprieve, remission*

veniō, venīre, vēnī, ventūrus, *to come*

ventus, -ī, m., *wind*

Venus, Veneris, f., *Venus* (goddess of love and Cupid's mother)

verbum, -ī, n., *word*

vereor, verērī, veritus sum, *to be afraid, fear*

Vergilius, -ī, m., *Vergil*

versō, -āre, -āvī, -ātus, *to turn, spin; to turn back and forth, twist*

versus, -ūs, m., *line* (of poetry or prose)

vertō, vertere, vertī, versus, *to* (cause to) *turn, spin; to reverse, change*

vērus, -a, -um, *true;* vērō, *truly*

vester, vestra, vestrum, *your* (pl.)

vestīgium, -ī, n., *track, footprint, trace*

vestis, vestis, f., *clothing, garment*

vetō, vetāre, vetuī, vetitus, *to forbid, tell not to*

vetus, veteris, *old*

via, -ae, f., *road, street*

viātor, viātōris, m., *traveler*

vīcīnus, -a, -um, *neighboring, adjacent; near, close*

victor, victōris, m., *conqueror, victor*

videō, vidēre, vīdī, vīsus, *to see*

vincō, vincere, vīcī, victus, *to win, conquer, overcome*

vinculum, -ī, n., *chain, shackle* (usually pl.)

vir, virī, m., *man*

virgō, virginis, f., *maiden*

vīs, vīs, f., *force;* pl. vīrēs, *strength*

vīta, -ae, f., *life*

vitium, -ī, n., *defect, fault; flaw, imperfection; vice*

vītō, -āre, -āvī, -ātus, *to avoid*

vitta, -ae, f., *ribbon, headband*

vīvō, vīvere, vīxī, vīctūrus, *to live*

vix, adv., *scarcely, with difficulty, only just*

vocō, -āre, -āvī, -ātus, *to call, invite*

volō, velle, voluī, irreg., *to wish, want, be willing*

volucer, volucris, f., *a winged creature, bird*

vōtum, -ī, n., *a vow; prayer, wish*

vōx, vōcis, f., *voice*

vulgus, -ī, m., *the common people, the multitude*

vulnus, vulneris, n., *wound*

vultus, -ūs, m., *face, expression*